SECRET
CODE
GAMES
for
Clever
Kids®

Puzzles and solutions
by Dr Gareth Moore
B.Sc (Hons) M.Phil Ph.D

Illustrations and cover
artwork by Chris Dickason

Designed by Tall Tree Ltd

SECRET CODE GAMES for Clever Kids

BUSTER BOOKS

First published in Great Britain in 2022 by Buster Books,
an imprint of Michael O'Mara Books Limited,
9 Lion Yard, Tremadoc Road, London SW4 7NQ

W   www.mombooks.com/buster

f   Buster Books

y   @BusterBooks

O   @buster_books

Clever Kids is a trade mark of Michael O'Mara Books Limited.

Puzzles and solutions © Gareth Moore

Illustrations and layouts © Buster Books 2022

A CIP catalogue record for this book is available from the British Library.

ISBN: 978-1-78055-873-8

3 5 7 9 10 8 6 4

This product is made of material from well-managed, FSC®-certified
forests and other controlled sources. The manufacturing processes
conform to the environmental regulations of the country of origin.

Printed and bound in October 2023 by
CPI Group (UK) Ltd, Croydon, CR0 4YY.

MIX
Paper | Supporting
responsible forestry
FSC® C171272

INTRODUCTION

Get ready to push your brain to the limit and challenge your intellect in this code-cracking adventure!

Take your pick of over 100 code-based puzzles. You can complete them in any order you like and work through at your own pace. Each puzzle gives you space to write down your answers and, when you're finished, you can check them against the solutions at the back.

Start each puzzle by reading the instructions. Sometimes this is the hardest part of the puzzle, so don't worry if you have to read the instructions a few times to be clear on what they mean. There is also a code guide at the back of the book to help you tackle some of the games.

INTRODUCTION

At the top of every page, there is a space for you to write how much time it took you to complete the puzzle on your first go. If you come back at a later date to try it again, you could then see if you've got faster at it.

If you really struggle with a puzzle, take a look at the solutions at the back to see how it works, then try it again later and see if you can do it the second time round.

Good luck, and have fun!

Introducing the Code Games Master:
Gareth Moore, B.Sc (Hons) M.Phil Ph.D
Dr Gareth Moore is a code-cracking genius, and author of lots of puzzle books.

He created an online brain-training site called BrainedUp.com, and runs a puzzle site called PuzzleMix.com. Gareth has a Ph.D from the University of Cambridge, where he taught machines to understand spoken English.

Numbers can be used to write secret codes. The simplest way to do this is with a numeric code where A is replaced with 1, B is replaced with 2, and so on – right up until Z = 26.

The full code looks like this:

A	B	C	D	E	F	G
1	2	3	4	5	6	7

H	I	J	K	L	M
8	9	10	11	12	13

N	O	P	Q	R	S	T
14	15	16	17	18	19	20

U	V	W	X	Y	Z
21	22	23	24	25	26

Use the code on the opposite page to decode the following
words, then read them from top to bottom to reveal a
secret message:

1)   20   1   11   5   ....

2)   20   8   5   ....

3)   20   18   1   9   14   ....

4)   20   8   18   5   5   ....

5)   19   20   15   16   19 ....

SECRET CODE GAME 2

⏰ TIME ....

Imagine mixing the two images together below, so that the blank squares in the left-hand image are filled with the corresponding pieces from the right-hand image.

What secret message is revealed?

....

Reveal a hidden secret message by rewriting the letters on each line in alphabetical order, placing them on the blank line next to each word.

1) OD ....

2) TON ....

3) TAPECC ....

4) NAY ....

5) SIBLL ....

First, read the 'Musical Codes' guide at the back of the book for an explanation of how to read the musical notes shown on this page.

The tune below conceals the location where a spy meet-up is taking place. Can you work out where it is by reading the musical note letters, from left to right? Use the guide at the back of the book to help you.

Write the secret message here:

....

First, read the 'Radio Codewords' guide at the back of the book for a list of radio codeword letters, and an explanation of how they work.

Decode each of these words, which have been written as if they were being spelled out with radio codewords. There is one word per line, but if you read all the words in order from top to bottom what secret message is revealed?

1) Yankee Oscar Uniform ....

2) Delta India Delta ....

3) Whiskey Echo Lima Lima ....

4) Whiskey India Tango Hotel ....

5) Tango Hotel India Sierra ....

6) Papa Uniform Zulu Zulu Lima Echo ....

Take a look at the sentences below, then continue on to the next page.

1) Try to keep an eye on one code at once

2) The balloon was blocking the pilot's view of the airport

3) My friend is a private swimming instructor

4) They drove the black car to my new house

5) The thieves stole a lot of valuable gold necklaces

6) The spy's coat had an invisible hood

Here are the same sentences as on the previous page, but with one word in each sentence changed.

Underline the altered words on this page, then read them from top to bottom to reveal a secret message.

1) Try to keep an eye on every code at once

2) The cloud was blocking the pilot's view of the airport

3) My friend has a private swimming instructor

4) They drove the black car to a new house

5) The thieves stole a lot of valuable silver necklaces

6) The spy's coat had an invisible lining

What does the secret message say?

....

....

One letter is missing from each of these animal names. Work out which letters have disappeared, then read them from top to bottom to spell out a secret word.

1) LIARD ....

2) RANGUTAN ....

3) PEACCK ....

4) OALA ....

5) ANTATER ....

6) ZBRA ....

7) ELEHANT ....

8) PNGUIN ....

9) TIGE ....

What is the secret word?

....

Hidden in the letter grid below is a secret message. Can you use the second grid to help you reveal it?

What does the secret message say? ....

....

SECRET CODE GAME 9 ⟶

⏱ TIME ....

Place A, C, E, R, S or T into each empty square so that no letter repeats in any row, column or bold-lined 3×2 box.

Once all the letters are placed, a hidden word can be read in the shaded diagonal from top to bottom.

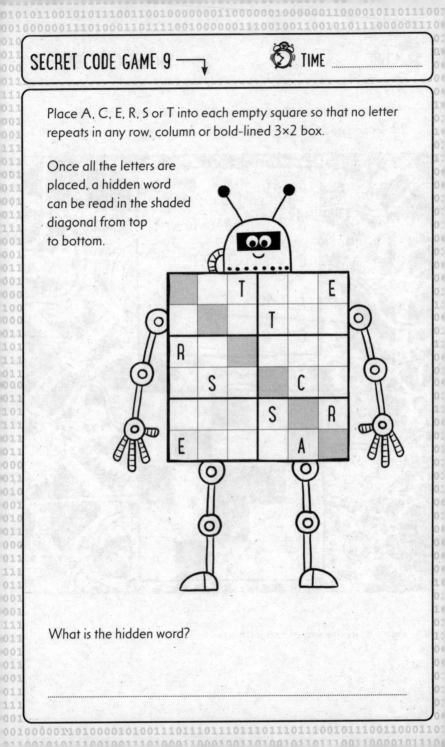

		T			E
			T		
R					
	S			C	
			S		R
E				A	

What is the hidden word?

....

Read the visually emphasized words in the passage below,
to reveal a secret message!

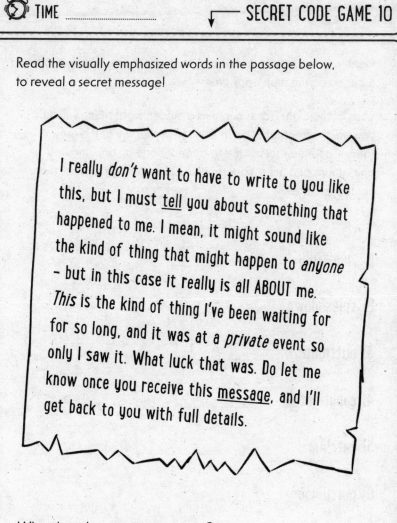

I really *don't* want to have to write to you like this, but I must <u>tell</u> you about something that happened to me. I mean, it might sound like the kind of thing that might happen to *anyone* – but in this case it really is all ABOUT me. *This* is the kind of thing I've been waiting for for so long, and it was at a *private* event so only I saw it. What luck that was. Do let me know once you receive this <u>message</u>, and I'll get back to you with full details.

What does the secret message say?

....

....

Hidden in this list of words are instructions to find where treasure is buried on the map opposite.

Each of the eight words **contains a hidden word which will tell you which direction to go in**. Start your journey at the grey square, and then follow the instructions one by one, moving one square at a time. Your path can pass through squares that contain pictures.

1) rightfully   ....

2) splashdown   ....

3) outrightly   ....

4) copyright   ....

5) ketchup   ....

6) porcupine   ....

7) bankrupt   ....

8) leftovers   ....

Which letter do you end up at: A, B or C? ....

Find as many of the following words in the word search grid as you can. They can run in any direction, including diagonally, and may read either forwards or backwards.

Some words, however, *cannot* be found in the grid! Read these leftover words in alphabetical order to reveal a secret message.

ABSOLUTE	BRING
CODE	CONTACT
EVERY	MESSAGE
MONDAY	PACKAGE
PURCHASE	SECRET
STORE	TEXT
THIS	THURSDAY
TOASTER	WEDNESDAY

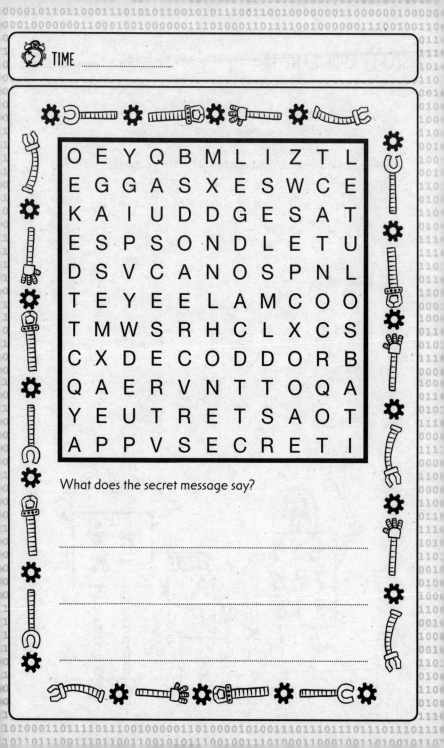

O	E	Y	Q	B	M	L	I	Z	T	L
E	G	G	A	S	X	E	S	W	C	E
K	A	I	U	D	D	G	E	S	A	T
E	S	P	S	O	N	D	L	E	T	U
D	S	V	C	A	N	O	S	P	N	L
T	E	Y	E	E	L	A	M	C	O	O
T	M	W	S	R	H	C	L	X	C	S
C	X	D	E	C	O	D	D	O	R	B
Q	A	E	R	V	N	T	T	O	Q	A
Y	E	U	T	R	E	T	S	A	O	T
A	P	P	V	S	E	C	R	E	T	I

What does the secret message say?

....

....

....

Each of these words has another word hidden inside it.
For example, 'LEVER' is hiding inside 'C**LEVER**LY'.

Can you find a hidden **number** in all of the following words?

1) Artwork ....

2) Braininess ....

3) Extent ....

4) Heights ....

5) Telephones ....

Starting at the grey square, can you work out how to use the following arrows to reveal a secret message hidden in the grid?

↑ → ↑ ← ↑ → → → ↓ ← ↓ → ↓ ← ←

T	H	E	P
D	N	N	I
F	I	K	F
	H	S	I

What does the secret message say?

....

....

⏱ TIME ....

The following short passage of text conceals the location at which a top-secret meeting will take place.

Can you read down the first letters of each line to reveal where this will be?

Brilliantly disguising messages
Using various methods
Successfully hides hidden text.

Simply take the initial letter
That you find on each of these lines
And you will soon discover
That the secret location
Is not so secret after all –
Only take care
Not to make any mistakes.

What is the secret location?

....

First, read the 'Braille' guide at the back of the book for a list of Braille letters, and an explanation of how they work.

Can you decode the following words that have been written in Braille, to reveal a relevant message? There is one word encoded on each line.

1) .... YOU ....

2) .... CAN ....

3) .... NOW ....

4) .... READ ....

5) .... IN ....

6) .... THE ....

7) .... DARK ....

SECRET CODE GAME 17 ⟶

⏱ TIME ....

Each of the words in the following sentences has been disguised in the same way. Work out what's happened to the words, then reveal the secret message hiding on each line.

1) reviled eht eton ot eht nam desserd ni der

....

2) ekam erus ydobon sees uoy

....

3) uoy lliw eb nevig a terces eman

....

4) uoy evah net setunim ot etelpmoc eht noissim

....

5) doog kcul htiw ruoy tnatropmi ksat

....

Each of the five rows below represents a letter of the alphabet, but they aren't using normal mathematics. Can you work out how to interpret each line, and then reveal the five-letter word?

As a hint, if the + and − signs aren't adding the numbers, what might they be adding or taking away?

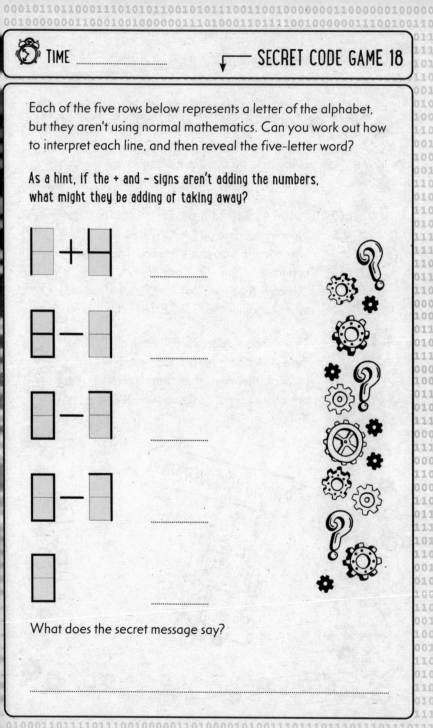

....

....

....

....

....

What does the secret message say?

....

Every time that you're looking for a secret message in some teXt, keep An eye out for randoMly caPitaLized tExt.

Now try reading all the CAPITAL letters in the previous sentence. The capital letters are 'E' (from 'Every'), 'X' (from 'teXt'), 'A', 'M', 'P', 'L', 'E', and taken together they spell EXAMPLE.

There's one hidden word in each of the following sentences. Can you find them all, then read them from top to bottom to reveal a secret message?

NOW LOOK OVER THERE

1) Monday morning – buy me an Easter Egg and bring it to me on Tuesday

....

2) Monday afternoon – and buy me an Easter cake too

....

3) And as a reminder, don't forget about Tuesday!

....

4) Tuesday is the day we attend Home Economics lessons

....

5) But Always remember to Never call me the 'King'!

....

What does the secret message say?

....

....

SECRET CODE GAME 20 ⟶

First, read the 'Radio Codewords' guide at the back of the book for a list of radio codeword letters, and an explanation of how they work.

Can you find a radio codeword hidden in each line, right? For example, 'ALFA' is hidden in 'I found the fin**al fa**lse message'.

Once you've found all the codewords, read them in order from top to bottom to reveal a secret word.

NOW LOOK OVER THERE

⏱ TIME ....

1) Are you travelling to Rome, or Madrid?

....

2) We chose the blue curtains.

....

3) Did the convict organize his own escape?

....

4) The screech owl made a loud noise!

....

5) The cow and her calf always eat grass.

....

6) Can you tell I'm a bit nervous?

....

What is the secret word? ....

SECRET CODE GAME 21 ⟶ TIME ....

Try reading just the first word in each sentence below,
to reveal a secret message! There is one hidden
sentence to discover per paragraph.

I am sending you a quick note. Have you had time
to read my previous one? Hidden inside it was
something just for you! The time you will take to
read it is well worth it. Cash this up to experience.
Under no circumstances must you show it to anyone
else, however! The message is too important. Plant
yourself somewhere comfortable before reading it.

You should then read this message next. Will you
promise me to do so? Find the time, even if you're
really busy. It is important. Just like you said you
would - remember? Inside every note is some hidden
text. The content that's just for you. Leaves nothing
for a nosy person to discover by chance, when I send
it like this!

What does the secret message say?

....

....

First, read the 'Semaphore' guide at the back of the book for a list of semaphore letters, and an explanation of how they work.

Reveal a secret message by decoding the following words written in semaphore. There is one word per line.

1) ....

2) ....

3) ....

4) ....

5) ....

6) ....

SECRET CODE GAME 23 ⟶   ⏱ TIME ....

Five items that are grown on trees have been disguised below by changing one letter in each word. For example, 'DRAPE' is 'GRAPE' in disguise, since the 'G' has been changed to a 'D'.

Reveal the disguised items, and make a note of what the incorrect letter should be changed to. Then read these 'changed to' letters in order from top to bottom, to reveal a relevant secret word.

1) **DIG** ....

2) **CHEERY** ....

3) **PRONE** ....

4) **LAME** ....

5) **DAZE** ....

What is the secret word?

....

Can you crack the code to reveal a hidden six-letter word?

Each word below is missing its first and last letters, which **must be the same** – as for example in the word **W**INDO**W**. For each word, work out which one letter has been removed from the start and end, and write it in. A clue to each word is given.

Once you have worked out which letter is needed for each line, read those letters in order from top to bottom to reveal the hidden word.

......**CARE**......   Frightens

......**NTIR**......   All, as in 'all of something'

......**OSMI**......   Relating to the universe in general

......**EPAI**......   Fix

......**DIBL**......   Okay to eat

......**EAPO**......   You can brew hot drinks in it

What is the hidden word? ....

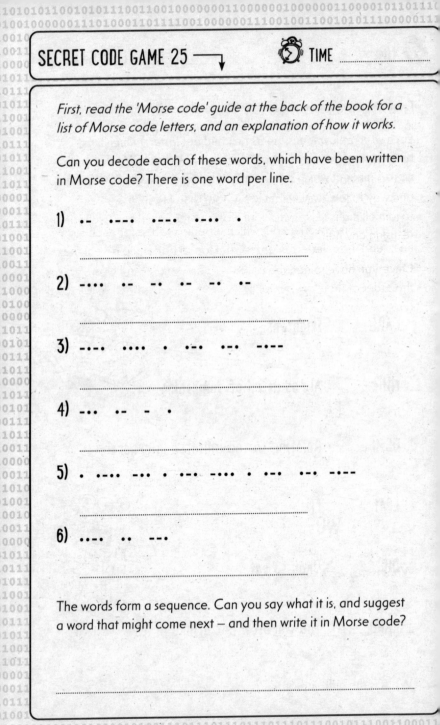

First, read the 'Morse code' guide at the back of the book for a list of Morse code letters, and an explanation of how it works.

Can you decode each of these words, which have been written in Morse code? There is one word per line.

1) .- .--. .--. .-.. .

....

2) -... .- -. .- -. .-

....

3) -.-. .... . .-. .-. -.--

....

4) -.. .- - .

....

5) . .-.. -.. . .-. -... . .-. .-. -.--

....

6) ..-. .. --.

....

The words form a sequence. Can you say what it is, and suggest a word that might come next – and then write it in Morse code?

....

Four words have been split in half, and their first halves placed in the left column and their second halves placed in the right column.

Match the halves back up to form four words. There is more than one way to join some of the parts together, but only one way to join all eight halves into four words at the same time, without re-using any half.

Once you have joined the pairs, read down the resulting words in the order of their left-hand halves, from top to bottom, to reveal a secret message.

FI	CH
EA	ND
TI	NY
WO	RD

What is the secret message?

....

....

SECRET CODE GAME 27 →

An ancient code, known as 'Atbash', involves reversing the
position of each letter in the alphabet – so that A becomes
Z, B becomes Y, and so on through until Z becomes A.

The full code looks like this:

A	B	C	D	E	F	G
Z	Y	X	W	V	U	T

H	I	J	K	L	M
S	R	Q	P	O	N

N	O	P	Q	R	S	T
M	L	K	J	I	H	G

U	V	W	X	Y	Z
F	E	D	C	B	A

Can you use Atbash to decode the following messages?

1) Nvvgrmt rh glmrtsg

....

2) Gsv kzhhdliw rh 'yzmzmzh'

....

3) Gzk gsivv grnvh lm gsv wlli

....

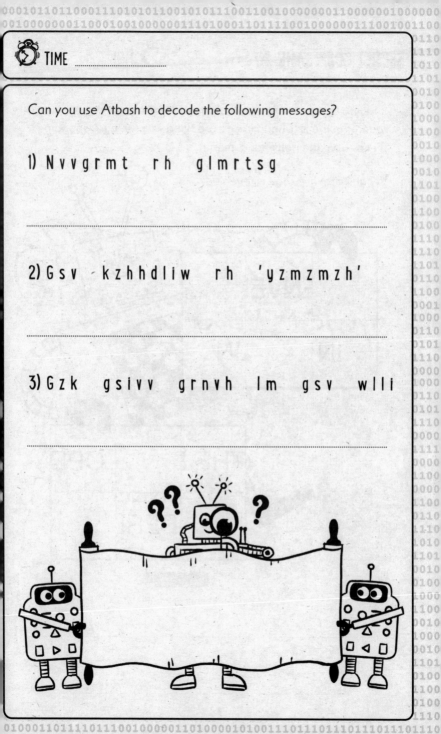

Imagine mixing the two images together below, so that the blank squares in the left-hand image are filled with the corresponding pieces from the right-hand image.

What secret message is revealed?

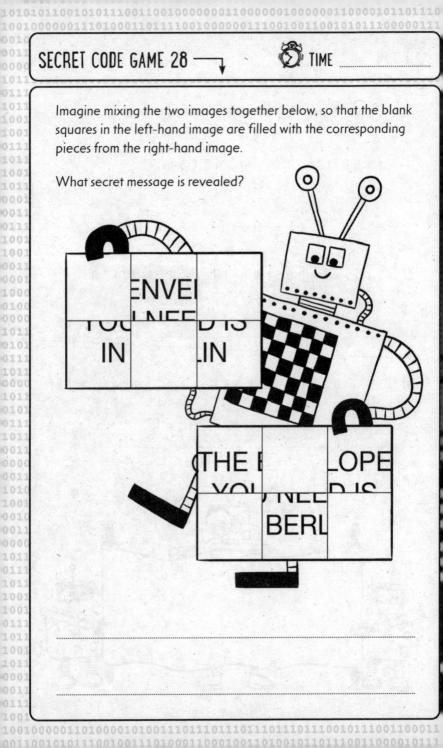

THE ENVELOPE
YOU NEED IS
IN BERLIN

....

....

All of the words on this page have been disguised at once using the same method. Can you work out what that method is, and then write down the four original words?

Once you've cracked the code, can you say what tool you could also have used to read them more easily?

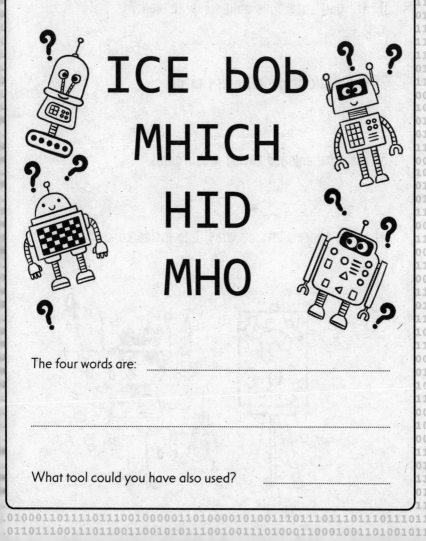

ICE ᏏOᏏ

MHICH

HID

MHO

The four words are: ....

....

What tool could you have also used? ....

Can you spot a shade of paint hidden in each of the lines below?
For example, the shade YELLOW can be found hidden in
'Don't **yell – ow**ls can't sleep if you're noisy!'.

1) Are you sure dogs only sleep at night?

....

2) The magic arrow hit every target.

....

3) The ogre enjoyed eating mushrooms.

....

4) When there's lots of wind, I go inside to keep warm.

....

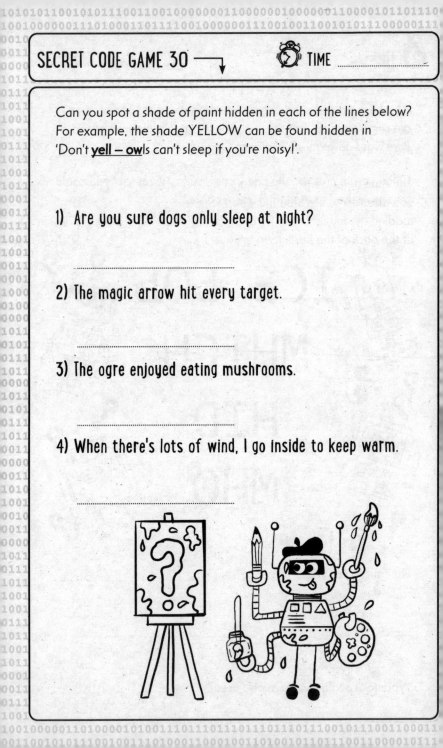

First, read the 'Musical Codes' guide at the back of the book for an explanation of how to read the musical notes shown on this page.

The tune below conceals something you'll need to wear when you attend a secret meeting. Can you work out what it is by reading the musical note letters, from left to right? Use the guide at the back of the book to help you.

What does the secret message say?

....

SECRET CODE GAME 32 ⟶

Numbers can be used to write secret codes. The simplest way to do this is with a numeric code where A is replaced with 1, B is replaced with 2, and so on – right up until Z = 26.

The full code looks like this:

A	B	C	D	E	F	G
1	2	3	4	5	6	7

H	I	J	K	L	M
8	9	10	11	12	13

N	O	P	Q	R	S	T
14	15	16	17	18	19	20

U	V	W	X	Y	Z
21	22	23	24	25	26

Decode the following words, then read them from top to bottom to reveal a secret message.

1) 23   5   1   18   ....

2) 1   ....

3) 2   12   21   5   ....

4) 18   9   2   2   15   14   ....

5) 20   15   4   1   25   ....

TIME ....

Place A, D, L, N, O or P into each empty square so that no letter repeats in any row, column or bold-lined 3×2 box.

Once, all the letters are placed, a hidden location can be read in the shaded diagonal from top to bottom.

	N			P	D
		D	N		
				A	O
A	P				L
N		L	A		
O	A			L	D

What is the hidden location?

....

Reveal a hidden secret message by rewriting the letters on each line in alphabetical order, placing them on the blank line next to each word.

1) THIN .... :

2) BEING ....

3) ELBOW .... ,

4) RIFTS ....

5) ROOD ....

First, read the 'Braille' guide at the back of the book for a list of Braille letters and an explanation of how they work.

Can you decode the following words that have been written in Braille, to reveal a relevant message? There is one word encoded on each line.

Each of the words in the following sentences has been disguised in the same way. Work out what's happened to the words, then reveal the secret message hiding on each line.

1) ocme ot hte fofice ebfore imdnight

....

2) hte enxt ubs ot rarive atkes oyu baroad

....

3) ermember ot ewar eyllow lgoves

....

4) amke usre veery upzzle ahs eben oslved

....

5) htis si hte ifnal ocde fo htis ytpe

....

0101011001010111001100100000011000001000001100001011011100
0010000001110100011011110010000001100100110010101100001110

Each of these words has a double agent hidden inside it.
Work out what is meant in this case by a 'double agent', and
then read the double agents from top to bottom to reveal a
hidden message.

Funny

Hawaii

Accept

Green

Three

Stuff

Puffy

Spoon

Berry

Better

What is the hidden message?

....

0010000011010000101001110111011101110111011100101100110001110
0110010101110010011101000110001001101001011011100110000101110

*First, read the 'Semaphore' guide at the back of the book for a
list of semaphore letters, and an explanation of how they work.*

Reveal a secret message by decoding the following words written
in semaphore. There is one word per line.

1) 🚩 🚩 🚩 ....

2) 🚩 🚩 ....

3) 🚩 🚩 🚩 🚩 ....

4) 🚩 🚩 🚩 🚩 ....

5) 🚩 🚩 🚩 🚩 ....

6) 🚩 🚩 🚩 🚩 🚩 ....

What does the secret message say?

....

....

One letter is missing from each of these country names. Work out which letters have disappeared, then read them from top to bottom to spell out a secret word.

1) CANDA ....

2) PORTGAL ....

3) PAIN ....

4) ARGENINA ....

5) ALGEIA ....

6) JPAN ....

7) VENEZUEA ....

8) THALAND ....

9) VIETNM ....

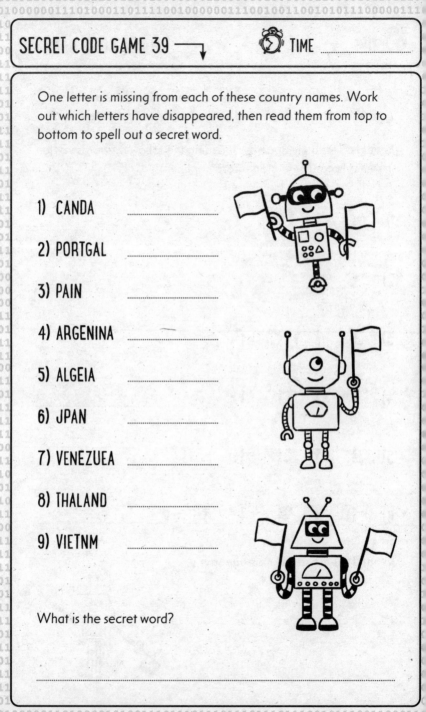

What is the secret word?

....

First, read the 'Morse code' guide at the back of the book for a list of Morse code letters, and an explanation of how it works.

Hidden in the punctuation in each line below is a Morse code letter, which you can reveal by reading the punctuation in order from left to right. For example, a line which had just two dashes would represent '– –', indicating the letter 'M'.

Reveal the Morse code letters, then read them from top to bottom to find a secret word.

1) I love pancakes. Waffles taste
   weird. Biscuits are okay. ....

2) Try not to run – there is very
   little space in the corridors ....

3) I live in a spaceship. I do like
   the view – but it is quite lonely. ....

4) I like all animals – except parrots
   – because they are so noisy –
   although they do look pretty ....

5) I love flying my kite – but not
   if it is a very windy day. ....

6) Some trees – like oak and horse
   chestnut trees – lose their leaves in the winter. ....

What is the secret word? ....

Take a look at the sentences below, then continue on to the next page.

1) The wind was so strong I couldn't close the window

2) I don't know how to drive a car

3) The woman was holding a bunch of yellow flowers

4) The gate at the bottom of the garden is locked

5) The suitcase was full of envelopes for coded letters

6) It took a long time to locate the secret agent

7) I need to take the bicycle in so I can repair it

Here are the same sentences as on the previous page, but with one word in each sentence changed.

Underline the altered words on <u>this</u> page, then read them from top to bottom to reveal a secret message.

1) The wind was so strong I couldn't open the window

2) I don't know how to drive the car

3) The woman was holding a bunch of green flowers

4) The door at the bottom of the garden is locked

5) The suitcase was full of envelopes and coded letters

6) It took a long time to find the secret agent

7) I need to take the bicycle out so I can repair it

What does the secret message say?

....

....

First, read the 'Radio Codewords' guide at the back of the book for a list of radio codeword letters, and an explanation of how they work.

Decode each of these words, which have been written as if they were being spelled out with radio codewords. There is one word per line, but if you read all the words in order from top to bottom what secret message is revealed?

1) Whiskey Alfa India Tango ....

2) Uniform November Tango India Lima ....

3) Tango Hotel Echo ....

4) Hotel India Golf Hotel ....

5) Sierra Papa Echo Echo Delta ....

6) Tango Romeo Alfa India November ....

7) Alfa Romeo Romeo India Victor Echo Sierra ....

What does the secret message say?

....

....

Each of these words has another word hidden inside it.
For example, 'LEVER' is hiding inside 'C**LEVER**LY'.

Can you find a hidden **animal** in all of the following words?

1) Locate   ....

2) Millions   ....

3) Resealed   ....

4) Growled   ....

5) Unselfishly   ....

Starting at the grey square, can you work out how to use the following letters to reveal a secret message hidden in the grid?

N N W S S W W N E N W N E E E

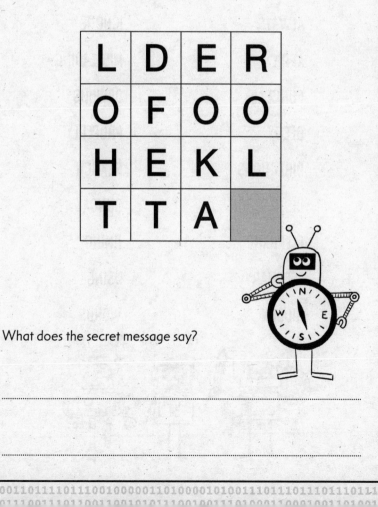

What does the secret message say?

....

....

Find as many of the following words in the word search grid as you can. They can run in any direction, including diagonally, and may read either forwards or backwards.

Some words, however, *cannot* be found in the grid! Read these leftover words in alphabetical order to reveal a secret message.

ALWAYS	IGNORE
APRIL	MISLEADING
CONCEAL	OBVIOUS
DECOY	PROPERLY
DIRECTIONS	SEARCH
DISTRACTION	SUNDAY
ELEPHANT	TIMING
FEBRUARY	USING
HIDDEN	WORDS

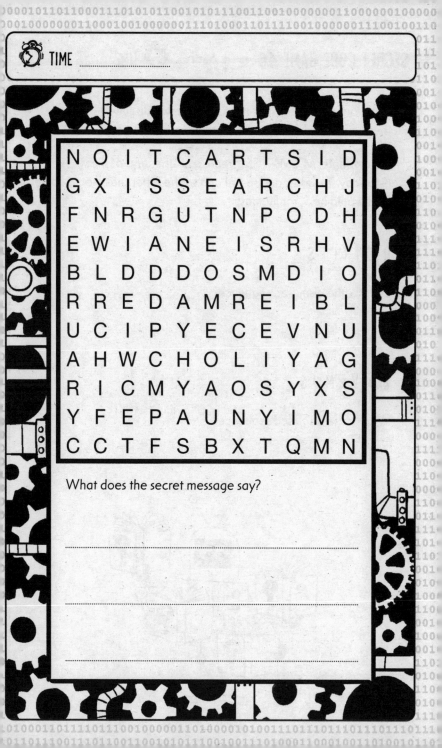

N	O	I	T	C	A	R	T	S	I	D
G	X	I	S	S	E	A	R	C	H	J
F	N	R	G	U	T	N	P	O	D	H
E	W	I	A	N	E	I	S	R	H	V
B	L	D	D	D	O	S	M	D	I	O
R	R	E	D	A	M	R	E	I	B	L
U	C	I	P	Y	E	C	E	V	N	U
A	H	W	C	H	O	L	I	Y	A	G
R	I	C	M	Y	A	O	S	Y	X	S
Y	F	E	P	A	U	N	Y	I	M	O
C	C	T	F	S	B	X	T	Q	M	N

What does the secret message say?

....

....

....

Can you identify each of the following two disguised sequences, then say which letter should come next in each case?

For example, M T W T F S _ represents the days of the week (**M**onday, **T**uesday, and so on) and so the letter that should come next would be S, for **S**unday.

1) O T T F F S _

What is the disguised sequence?

....

2) M V E M J S _

What is the disguised sequence?

....

Five words have been split in half, and their first halves placed in the left column and their second halves placed in the right column. Match the halves back up, forming all five words without re-using any half. Be careful, since there are some incorrect matches that do form valid words but which won't let you complete the other words.

LO	ES
WI	LY
YO	OK
EY	TH
ON	UR

What does the secret message say?

....

....

Each line below is missing a hidden word, which can be written in the middle column. This word can join to the end of the word to its left, and join to the start of the word to its right, to make two new words.

For example, 'SUN _ _ _ _ _ _ POT' is hiding the word 'FLOWER' in the middle, making SUNFLOWER and FLOWERPOT. The number of underlines shows the number of letters, and some letters are given to help you.

Find all five secret words, then read them from top to bottom to reveal a hidden message.

1)	OVER	L _ _ K	ALIKE
2)	HIDE	O _ T	SIDE
3)	GOLD	_ IS _	BOWL
4)	WITH	_ _	DEED
5)	RAIN	W _ T _ _	FALL

Each of the six rows below represents a letter of the alphabet, but they aren't using normal mathematics. Can you work out how to interpret each line, and then reveal the six-letter word?

As a hint, if the + and – signs aren't adding the numbers, what might they be adding or taking away?

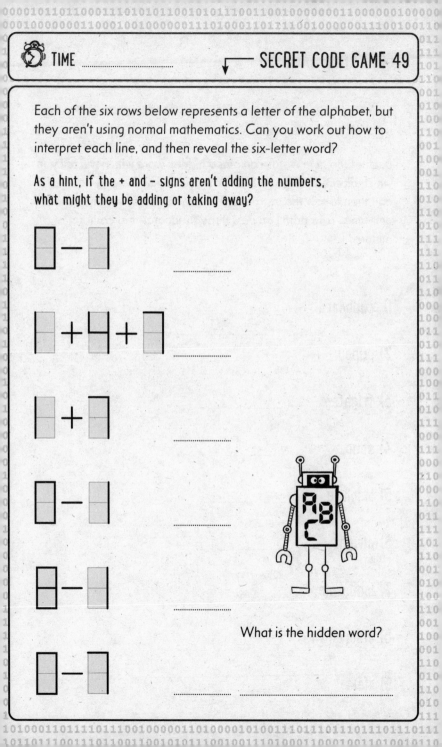

What is the hidden word?

....

Hidden in this list of words are instructions to find where treasure is buried on the map opposite.

Each of the nine words **contains a hidden word which will tell you which direction to go in**. Start your journey at the grey square, and then follow the instructions one by one, moving one square at a time. Your path can pass through squares that contain pictures.

1) cupboard ....

2) puppy ....

3) frighten ....

4) soup ....

5) brightly ....

6) alright ....

7) landowner ....

8) eiderdown ....

9) cleft ....

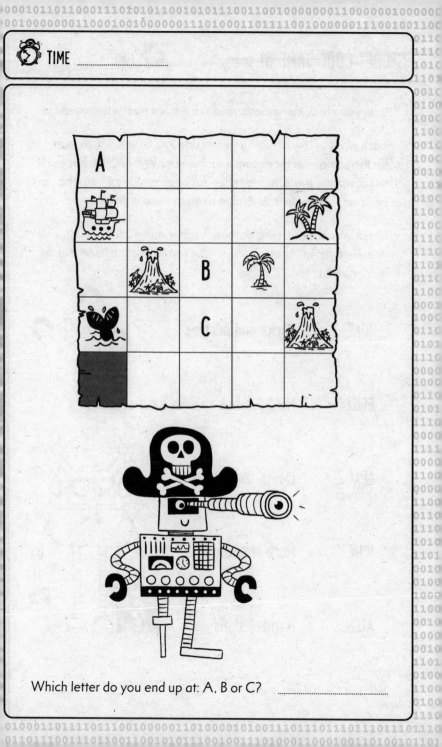

Which letter do you end up at: A, B or C? ....

⏱ TIME ....

Can you crack the code to reveal a hidden five-letter word?

Each word below is missing its first and last letters, which **must be the same** – as for example in the word <u>W</u>INDO<u>W</u>. For each word, work out which one letter has been removed from the start and end, and write it in. A clue to each word is given.

Once you have worked out which letter is needed for each line, read those letters in order from top to bottom to reveal the hidden word.

....TONE....   Rocks and pebbles

....EDIU....   Middle-sized, like an item of clothing

....LPAC....   Llama-like animal

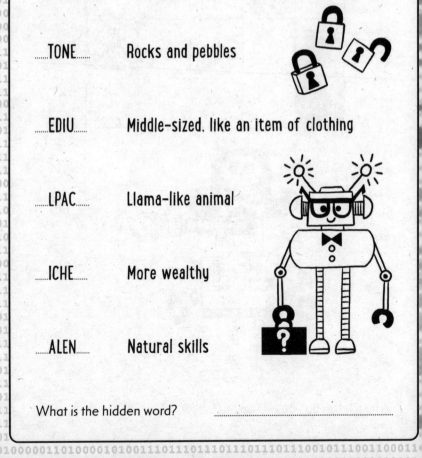

....ICHE....   More wealthy

....ALEN....   Natural skills

What is the hidden word? ....

First, read the 'Morse code' guide at the back of the book for a list of Morse code letters, and an explanation of how it works.

Can you decode each of these words, which have been written in Morse code? There is one word per line.

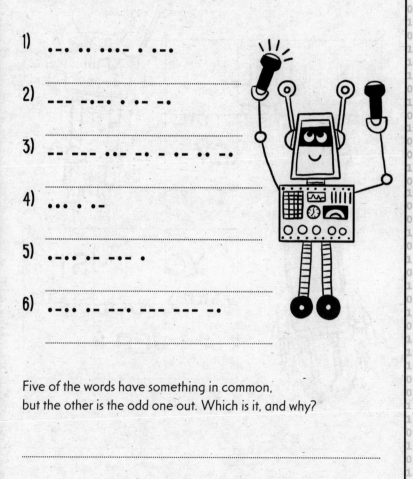

1) .-- .. ...- . .--

....

2) --- -.-. . .- -.

....

3) -- --- .-.. -.- - .. -.

....

4) ... . .--

....

5) .-.. .- -.- .

....

6) .-.. .- --. --- --- -.

....

Five of the words have something in common, but the other is the odd one out. Which is it, and why?

....

....

Imagine mixing the two images together below, so that the blank squares in the left-hand image are filled with the corresponding pieces from the right-hand image.

What secret message is revealed?

U MU

ONLY USE THE

SIL   KEY

YO   JST

ONLY   USE THE

VER K

....

....

First, read the 'Radio Codewords' guide at the back of the book for a list of radio codeword letters, and an explanation of how they work.

Decode each of these words, which have been written as if they were being spelled out with radio codewords. There is one word per line, and all of the words have something in common — except for one.

1) Echo Yankee Echo

....

2) Lima Echo Victor Echo Lima

....

3) Romeo Alfa Delta Alfa Romeo

....

4) November Oscar Oscar November

....

5) Hotel Echo Lima Lima Oscar

....

6) Kilo Alfa Yankee Alfa Kilo

....

Can you spot the odd one out, and say why?

....

....

Reveal a hidden secret message by rewriting the letters on each line in alphabetical order, placing them on the blank line next to each word.

1) SMALTO   ....

2) TOG   ....

3) SLOT   ....

4) NI   ....

5) LILYCH   ....

6) SHILL   ....

What has happened to each of the following words to disguise it? Can you read all three words in order to reveal a hidden message?

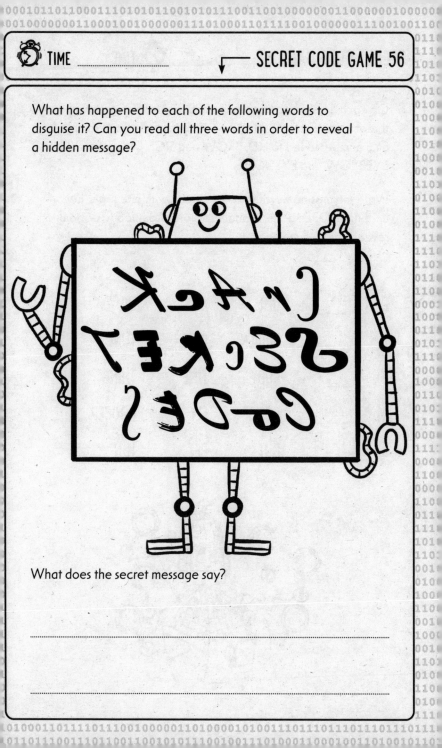

What does the secret message say?

....

....

On each line below, one word can be added in front of all three words to create three new, longer words. For example, EYE can be added to LID, BROW and SIGHT to make EYELID, EYEBROW and EYESIGHT.

Write the missing words into the spaces, with one letter per underline. Once done, read these words from top to bottom to reveal a hidden message.

1) _ _ _ _   OUT   ALIKE   UP

2) _ _ _   BIDDEN   GIVE   TUNE

3) _ _ _   BODY   TIME   THING

4) _ _ _ _ _ _   HOUSE   FLY   GROCER

5) _ _ _   ROT   PET   TON

First, read the 'Braille' guide at the back of the book for a list of Braille letters, and an explanation of how they work.

On each line below, imagine laying the two sets of dots one on top of the other. What Braille letter would result?

For example, laying the two dot patterns shown here would create the dot pattern on the right, which represents the letter 'L' in Braille:

$$\begin{matrix}•&○\\•&○\\○&○\end{matrix} \quad + \quad \begin{matrix}•&○\\○&○\\•&○\end{matrix} \quad = \quad \begin{matrix}•&○\\•&○\\•&○\end{matrix}$$

Once you've worked out all five letters, read them from top to bottom to reveal a hidden word.

1) $\begin{matrix}•&○\\•&•\\•&○\end{matrix} + \begin{matrix}•&○\\•&•\\○&○\end{matrix} = $ ....

2) $\begin{matrix}•&•\\○&○\\•&○\end{matrix} + \begin{matrix}•&•\\○&•\\○&○\end{matrix} = $ ....

3) $\begin{matrix}•&○\\○&○\\•&•\end{matrix} + \begin{matrix}○&○\\○&○\\○&•\end{matrix} = $ ....

4) $\begin{matrix}•&•\\○&○\\○&○\end{matrix} + \begin{matrix}•&•\\•&○\\○&○\end{matrix} = $ ....

5) $\begin{matrix}•&•\\○&○\\○&○\end{matrix} + \begin{matrix}•&•\\•&○\\○&○\end{matrix} = $ ....

What does the secret word say? ....

SECRET CODE GAME 59 →

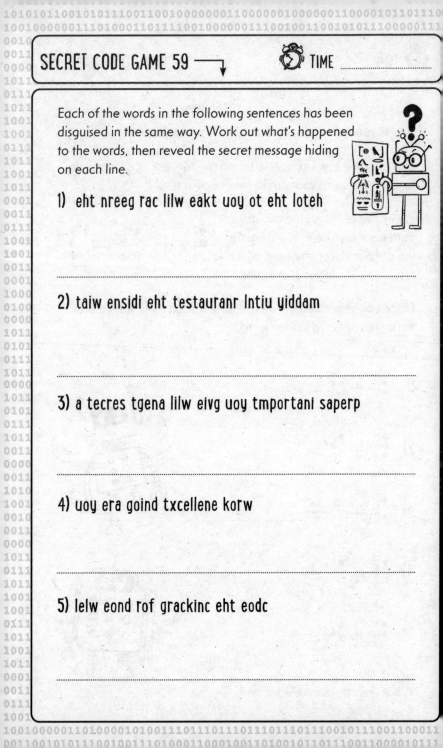

⏱ TIME ....

Each of the words in the following sentences has been
disguised in the same way. Work out what's happened
to the words, then reveal the secret message hiding
on each line.

1) eht nreeg rac lilw eakt uoy ot eht loteh

....

2) taiw ensidi eht testauranr lntiu yiddam

....

3) a tecres tgena lilw eivg uoy tmportani saperp

....

4) uoy era goind txcellene korw

....

5) lelw eond rof grackinc eht eodc

....

Six vehicles have been disguised below by changing one letter in each word. For example, 'BAR' is 'CAR' in disguise, since the 'C' has been changed to a 'B'.

Reveal the disguised vehicles, and make a note of what the incorrect letter should be changed to. Then read these 'changed to' letters in order from top to bottom to reveal a relevant secret word.

1) MAXI ....

2) TEAM ....

3) COUCH ....

4) BAN ....

5) PLANT ....

6) TRAINER ....

What is the secret word?

....

SECRET CODE GAME 61 ⟶

⏰ TIME ....

On each line, subtract all of the letters found in the second word from the first word, to leave just one letter. Then, read those remaining letters in order from top to bottom to reveal a secret word.

For example, DOG – GO = D, since the 'G' and 'O' are removed from 'DOG' to leave just the 'D'.

1) STAR – **ART** = ...

2) PEARL – **REAL** = ...

3) TEASING – **AGENTS** = ...

4) HEADS – **DASH** = ...

5) STABLE – **BLEAT** = ...

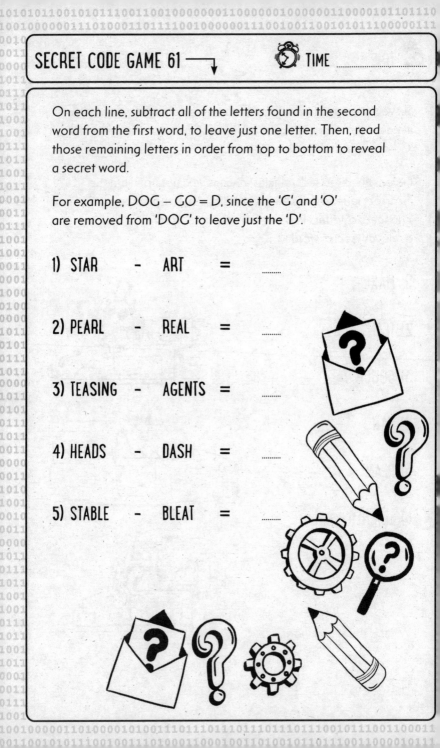

Four shades of paint – each of which has four letters in its name – have been secretly encoded in the block of letters below. Can you crack the code and reveal all four shades?

```
B P G C
L I O Y
U N L A
E K D N
```

⏲ TIME ....

First, read the 'Caesar shift' guide at the back of the book for an explanation of what a Caesar shift code is.

Each of the secret messages below has been encoded with a different size of Caesar shift to all the others. By experimenting with different shifts, can you decode each message? The alphabet is printed below to help, and as a clue you will need to shift each letter backwards through the alphabet to decode it – but never by more than 5 letters.

1) Gjoe uif xpnbo xjui uif sfe ibu

....

2) Brx duh dq hafhoohqw frgh fudfnhu

....

3) Jcppcj ku pqv oa tgcn pcog

....

4) M pmoi xs xvezip erh wspzi qcwxivmiw

....

A B C D E F G H I J K L M N O P Q R S T U V W X Y Z

First, read the 'Musical Codes' guide at the back of the book for an explanation of how to read the musical notes shown on this page.

The tune below conceals an item in which a secret message will be delivered to you. Can you work out what it is by reading the musical note letters, from left to right?

What does the secret message say?

....

Each of the rows of shapes below represents a four-letter word.
Can you crack the code, and reveal the two four-letter words?

As a hint, take a look at puzzle 1, and think about how this might
be used with these three shapes below, representing C, D and E.

C = △   D = ▢   E = ⬠

1)

----

2)

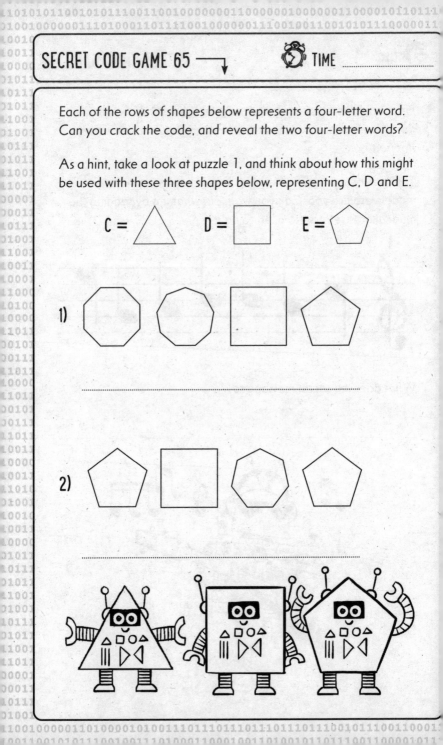

First, read the 'Radio Codewords' guide at the back of the book for a list of radio codeword letters, and an explanation of how they work.

Can you find a radio codeword hidden in each line below?
For example, 'ALFA' is hidden in 'I found the fin**al fa**lse message'.

Once you've found all the codewords, read them in order from top to bottom to reveal a secret word.

1) We stopped to help a pair of old ladies.

....

2) The sports hotshot elbowed his teammate.

....

3) I dreamed I saw two flamingos carrying handbags.

....

4) Which way did the orangutan go?

....

5) I don't want to scare the new puppy.

....

What does the secret word say? ....

Six words have been split in half, and their first halves placed
in the left column and their second halves placed in the right
column. Match the halves back up, forming all six words without
re-using any half. Be careful, since there are some incorrect
matches that do form valid words but which won't let you
complete the other words.

ALW   AYS

DEC   ILS

EMA   INE

DUR   ING

ONL   ODE

QUE   STS

What does the secret message say?

....

....

Place A, D, E, I, L, R, S, T or V into each empty square so that no letter repeats in any row, column or bold-lined 3×3 box.

Once all the letters are placed, a hidden word can be read in the shaded diagonal from top to bottom.

	S	R		E	V			L
V		T	L	I			S	
A	I			R		E		
	T			D	L			E
S	L	E	R		A	D		I
I			S	T		L	R	
		S		L	I		A	T
	R				T	V		S
T			E	S		I	L	

What is the hidden word?

....

One letter is missing from each of these vehicles. Work out which letters have disappeared, then read them from top to bottom to spell out a secret word.

1) RAIN   ....

2) CA   ....

3) BOT   ....

4) UICYCLE   ....

5) HIP   ....

6) LANE   ....

7) SCOTER   ....

8) FERY   ....

9) RAM   ....

What is the secret word?

....

First, read the 'Morse code' guide at the back of the book for a list of Morse code letters, and an explanation of how it works.

Can you decode each of these words, which have been written in Morse code? There is one word per line.

1) --- -.-. - --- .--. ..- ...

....

2) .--- . -... .-.. -.-- ..-. .. ..

....

3) ... .- .-. -.-

....

4) -- ....-.. .

....

5) . .. -- .-.. .

....

6) .-.. --- -... ... - . .-.

....

Five of the words have something in common, but the other is the odd one out. Which is it, and why?

....

....

Take a look at the sentences below, then continue on to the next page.

1) Did you eat a chocolate cookie?

2) I took a boat from Australia to New Zealand

3) What time did the guests arrive at the hotel?

4) The scientist was the smartest woman in the country

5) The post is usually delivered by midday

6) There were several giraffes in the local zoo

7) Thursday is the first day of the museum exhibition

8) Nocturnal animals have a hard time waking up in the evening

Here are the same sentences as on the previous page, but with one word in each sentence changed.

Underline the altered words on <u>this</u> page, then read them from top to bottom to reveal a secret message.

1) Did you eat the chocolate cookie?

2) I took a plane from Australia to New Zealand

3) What time will the guests arrive at the hotel?

4) The scientist was the smartest woman in the land

5) The post is usually delivered at midday

6) There were six giraffes in the local zoo

7) Tomorrow is the first day of the museum exhibition

8) Nocturnal animals have a hard time waking up in the morning

What does the secret message say?

....

....

Can you spot a flower hidden in each of the lines below? As an example, ROSE can be found hidden in 'The he**ro se**es the monster from miles away'.

1) The anaconda is yellowy-brown, with dark spots.

....

2) The armchair I sit in at the library is really comfy.

....

3) Is there any broccoli lying in the shopping basket?

....

4) Don't bring a torch – I don't think you'll need one.

....

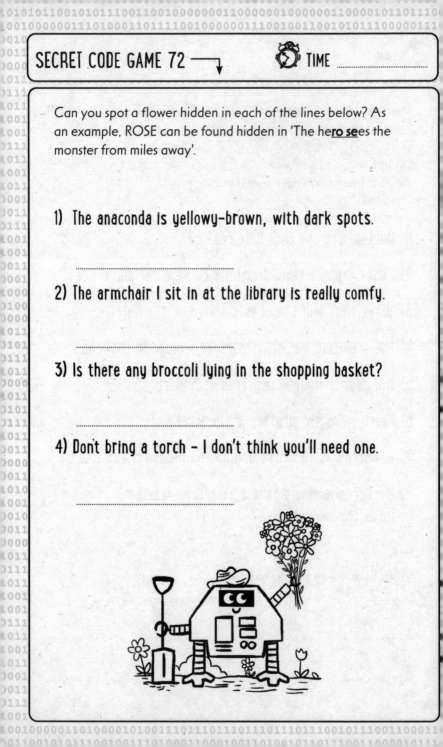

On each line below, one word can be added in front of all three words to create three new, longer words. For example, EYE can be added to LID, BROW and SIGHT to make EYELID, EYEBROW and EYESIGHT.

Write the missing words into the spaces, with one letter per underline. Once done, read these words from top to bottom to reveal a hidden message.

1) _ _ _   KING   SAW   MED

2) _ _ _ _   BERRY   BIRD   BELL

3) _ _ _ _   MARK   SHELF   CASE

4) _ _ _ _ _ _ WATER   STAND   COVER

5) _ _ _ _   LADDER   BROTHER   MOTHER

SECRET CODE GAME 74 ⟶

First, read the 'Semaphore' guide at the back of the book for a list of semaphore letters, and an explanation of how they work.

Some pairs of semaphore signals are mirror images of one another. For example, the signal for 'O' is a reflection of the signal for 'W':

O ◆🧍 ┊ 🧍◆ W

For each given letter opposite, draw the missing flags on to the person on the left as though they were giving the signal for that letter. Next, on the right, draw the mirror image of the figure you have just drawn. Then, finally, work out which letter that mirror image represents.

1) C

2) G

3) M

4) Q

Read the four new letters from top to bottom
to uncover a hidden word.

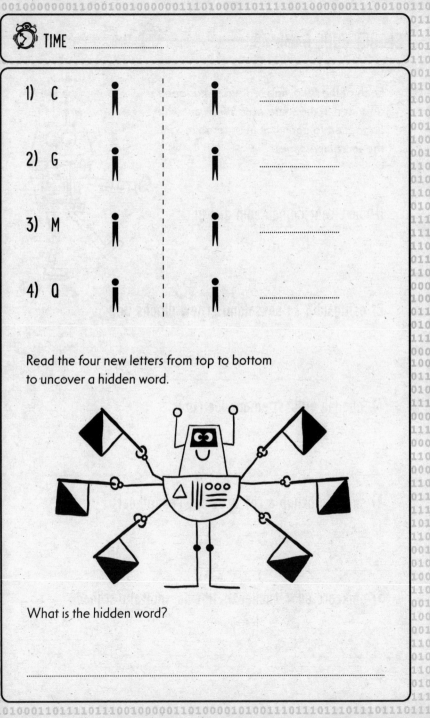

What is the hidden word?

....

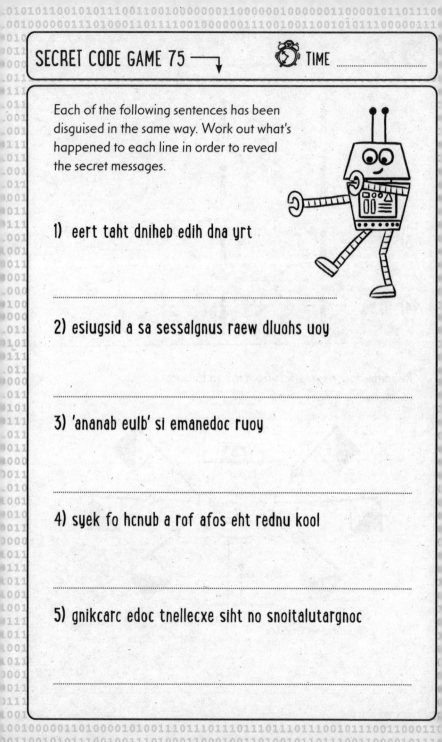

⏱ TIME ....

Each of the following sentences has been disguised in the same way. Work out what's happened to each line in order to reveal the secret messages.

1) eert taht dniheb edih dna yrt

....

2) esiugsid a sa sessalgnus raew dluohs uoy

....

3) 'ananab eulb' si emanedoc ruoy

....

4) syek fo hcnub a rof afos eht rednu kool

....

5) gnikcarc edoc tnellecxe siht no snoitalutargnoc

....

Can you identify each of the following two disguised sequences, then say which letter should come next in each case?

For example, M T W T F S _ represents the days of the week (**M**onday, **T**uesday, and so on) and so the letter that should come next would be S, for **S**unday.

1) R O Y G B I _

What is the disguised sequence?

....

2) J F M A M J _

What is the disguised sequence?

....

⏱ TIME ....

You've seen codes that use numbers to represent letters, but we can also use numbers to *extract* letters from other words.

In the sentences below, take the letter from each word that is indicated by each number in turn. So for example if you have the numbers '**1 4**' and the words 'Order book', you would take letter 1 from 'Order', which is 'O', and letter 4 from 'book', which is 'k', to spell 'Ok'.

Can you find the hidden word in each sentence below? Read them in order to reveal a secret message.

1 16 16 2 1 7 7 6 1 4 1 5 1 1 5 3 2 1 2 1 3 1 6

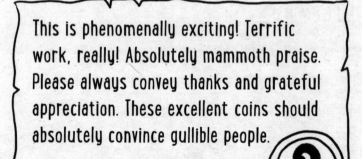

> This is phenomenally exciting! Terrific work, really! Absolutely mammoth praise. Please always convey thanks and grateful appreciation. These excellent coins should absolutely convince gullible people.

What does the secret message say?

....

....

Can you crack the code to reveal a hidden five-letter word?

Each word below is missing its first and last letters, which **must be the same** – as for example in the word **W**INDO**W**. For each word, work out which one letter has been removed from the start and end, and write it in. A clue to each word is given.

Once you have worked out which letter is needed for each line, read those letters in order from top to bottom to reveal the hidden word.

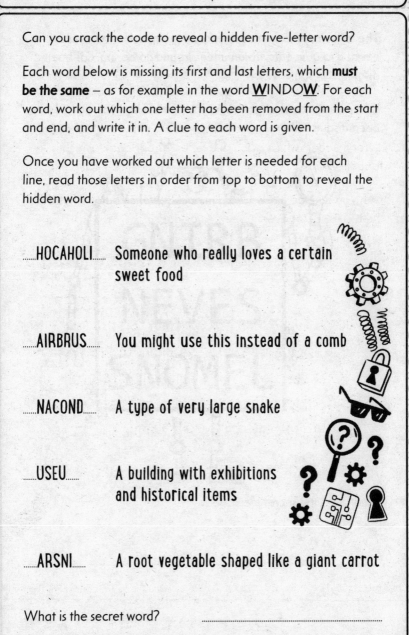

.....HOCAHOLI..... Someone who really loves a certain sweet food

.....AIRBRUS..... You might use this instead of a comb

.....NACOND..... A type of very large snake

.....USEU..... A building with exhibitions and historical items

.....ARSNI..... A root vegetable shaped like a giant carrot

What is the secret word? ....

The following secret message, giving instructions on what is needed to gain entry to an underground gathering, has been disguised in some way.

Can you work out what it says, and explain how the words have been disguised?

What does the secret message say?

....

....

Each of the six rows below represents a letter of the alphabet, but they aren't using normal mathematics. Can you work out how to interpret each line, and then reveal the six-letter word?

As a hint, if the + and – signs aren't adding the numbers, what might they be adding or taking away?

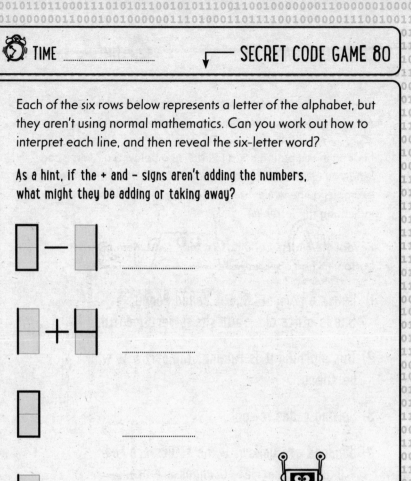

What is the hidden word?

....

First, read the 'Morse code' guide at the back of the book for a list of Morse code letters, and an explanation of how it works.

Hidden in the punctuation in each line below is a Morse code letter, by reading the punctuation in order from left to right. For example, a line which had just two dashes would represent '– –', indicating the letter 'M'.

Reveal the Morse code letters, then read them from top to bottom to find a secret word.

1) I have a pet cat. She is called Peggy.
   She is quite old – but she is very playful.   ....

2) This morning it is raining. Tomorrow it will
   be sunny.   ....

3) Solving codes is cool.   ....

4) Bananas are yellow. Some fruits are red
   – like strawberries. Oranges are orange.   ....

5) I can ride a bike – I learned when I
   was small. I like skateboarding too.   ....

What does the secret word say?

....

On each line, subtract all of the letters found in the second word from the first word, to leave just one letter. Then, read those remaining letters in order from top to bottom to reveal a secret word.

For example, DOG – GO = D, since the 'G' and 'O' are removed from 'DOG' to leave just the 'D'.

1) MAILED – IDEAL = ...

2) GRAIN – RANG = ...

3) HORSE – HERO = ...

4) SINGER – REIGN = ...

5) ADMIRE – DREAM = ...

6) LISTEN – TILES = ...

7) BADGER – BREAD = ...

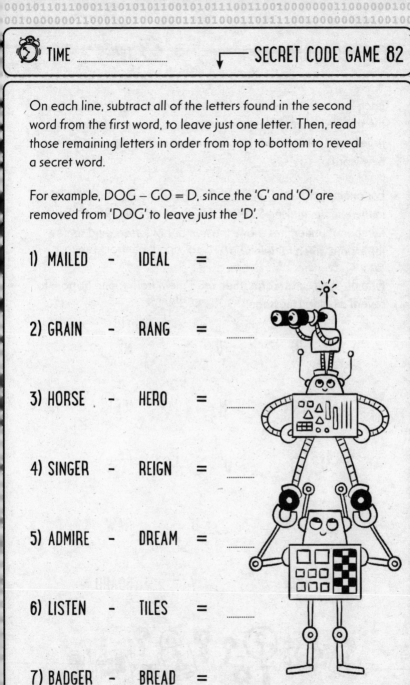

SECRET CODE GAME 83 →

 TIME ....

Each line below is missing a hidden word, which can be written in the middle column. This word can join to the end of the word to its left, and join to the start of the word to its right, to make two new words.

For example, 'SUN _ _ _ _ _ _ POT' is hiding the word 'FLOWER' in the middle, making SUNFLOWER and FLOWERPOT. The number of underlines shows the number of letters, and some letters are given to help you.

Find all five secret words, then read them from top to bottom to reveal a hidden message.

1)	UN	D _	ME
2)	CAN	N _ T	ICE
3)	REF	U _ _	LESS
4)	COVE	_ _ D	RAW
5)	DON	_ _ Y	BOARD

First, read the 'Morse code' guide at the back of the book for a list of Morse code letters, and an explanation of how it works.

Morse code can be sent in lots of different ways, such as by short and long sounds, or even short and long flashes of light. Another method is to use specific words, such as 'dot' and 'dash'.

Looking at the words 'dot' and 'dash' below, can you find a secret letter in each sentence – and then put them together in order to reveal a hidden password?

1) Time to dash to the park to meet Dot, who will be there on the dot of 1 o'clock I imagine – good old Dot! ....

2) Dot is always so reliable, dash it all. There on the dot she really was. ....

3) 'Today is going to be a good day,' Dot said to me. ....

4) Dot then had to dash home, which was a shame. ....

5) 'Dash!' I said – I'm sorry about that, Dot. But Dot was already gone. ....

What is the hidden password?

....

Each of the rows of shapes below represents a word.
Can you crack the code, and reveal the two words?

If you're stuck, take a look at the hints on puzzle 65.

1)

....

2)

....

Imagine mixing the two images together below, so that the blank squares in the left-hand image are filled with the corresponding pieces from the right-hand image.

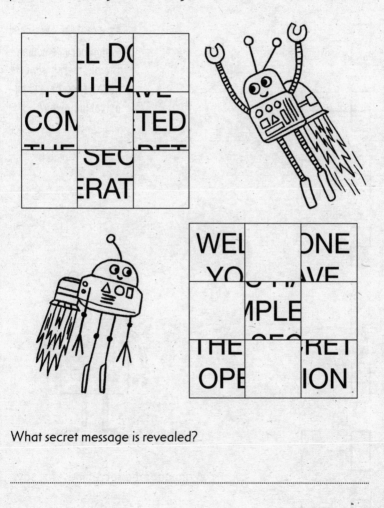

What secret message is revealed?

....

....

Each of the six rows below represents a letter of the alphabet, but they aren't using normal mathematics. Can you work out how to interpret each line, and then reveal the eight-letter word?

As a hint, if the + and – signs aren't adding the numbers, what might they be adding or taking away?

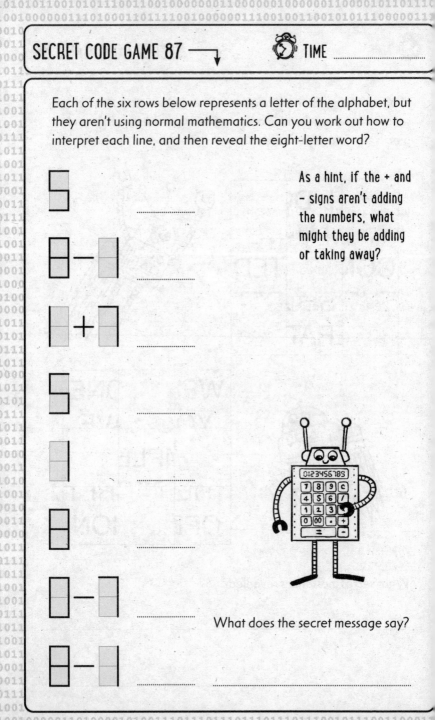

What does the secret message say?

First, read the 'Radio Codewords' guide at the back of the book for a list of radio codeword letters, and an explanation of how they work.

Decode each of these words, which have been written as if they were being spelled out with radio codewords. There is one word per line, and all of the words have something in common – except for one.

1) Romeo Echo Delta ....

2) Delta Echo Alfa Romeo ....

3) Alfa Delta Oscar Romeo Echo ....

4) Sierra Oscar Alfa Romeo
   Echo Delta ....

5) Romeo Oscar Alfa Sierra
   Tango Echo Delta ....

6) Alfa Sierra Tango Echo
   Romeo Oscar India Delta ....

7) Delta Romeo Echo Alfa Mike
   India Echo Sierra Tango ....

Can you spot the odd one out, and say why?

....

SECRET CODE GAME 89 → ⏱ TIME ....

Place A, B, D, E, O, R, S, T and V into each empty square so that no letter repeats in any row, column or bold-lined 3×3 box.

Once all the letters are placed, a hidden word can be read in the shaded diagonal from top to bottom.

	E				D		T	R
D	B	T	A		R		E	O
	R		O	E		V		
	D	O		T	S	R	A	B
		E	D		O			
S	T		B	A		D		E
		D	T		B		V	A
E	S		V			O		T
T	V		R		E	B	D	

What is the hidden word?

....

First, read the 'Morse code' guide at the back of the book for a list of Morse code letters, and an explanation of how it works.

Can you decode each of these words, which have been written in Morse code? There is one word per line.

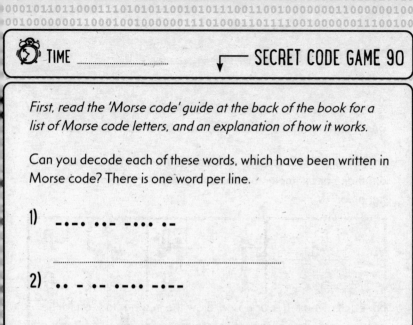

1) -.-. ..- -... .-

....

2) .. - .- .-.. -.--

....

3) ..-. .-. .- -. -.-. .

....

4) -... --- .-.. .. ...- .. .-

....

5) .--. .- .-. .- --. ... .- -.--

....

6) .. -. -.. --- -. . ...-

....

The words form a sequence. Can you say what it is, and suggest a word that might come next – and then write it in Morse code?

....

First, read the 'Semaphore' guide at the back of the book for a list of semaphore letters, and an explanation of how they work.

Some pairs of semaphore signals are mirror images of one another. For example, the signal for 'O' is a reflection of the signal for 'W':

O | W

For each given letter opposite, draw the missing flags on to the person on the left as though they were giving the signal for that letter. Next, on the right, draw the mirror image of the figure you have just drawn. Then, finally, work out which letter that mirror image represents.

1) M    | ....

2) X

3) A

4) N

Read the four new letters from top to bottom to uncover a hidden word.

What is the hidden word?

....

SECRET CODE GAME 92 ⟶

First, read the 'Braille' guide at the back of the book for a list of Braille letters, and an explanation of how they work.

On each line with a '+' sign opposite, imagine laying the two Braille characters representing each letter on top of one another. For example, laying the letter B on top of the letter K would result in the letter L:

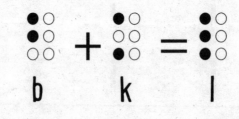

b + k = l

For each line with a '-' sign, imagine *removing* the dots shown in the Braille character on the right from the Braille character on the left.

For each line, which Braille character would result – and what is its corresponding letter? Once you've revealed all six letters, read them from top to bottom to reveal a hidden word.

1) b + i = ...

2) f – a = ...

3) k + d = ...

4) a + j = ...

5) g – i = ...

6) b + o = ...

What does the secret word say? ....

You've already seen a code where numbers become letters, back in the very first puzzle in the book. Based on that earlier code, can you work out what secret message is being represented by the following set of sums?

1 + 2   14 – 2   2 + 3   21 + 1   7 – 2   9 + 9

....

15 + 4   20 – 5   7 + 5   11 × 2   4 + 5   2 × 7   1 × 7

....

What does the secret message say?

....

One letter is missing from each of these capital cities. Work out which letters have disappeared, then read them from top to bottom to spell out a secret word.

1) ATHNS   ....

2) BDAPEST   ....

3) MADID   ....

4) LNDON   ....

5) ARIS   ....

6) ROM   ....

7) COPENHGEN ....

8) VIENA   ....

What is the secret word?

....

First, read the 'Caesar Shift' guide at the back of the book for an explanation of what a Caesar shift code is.

Each of the secret messages below has been encoded with a **different** size of Caesar shift to all the others. By experimenting with different shifts, can you decode each message? The alphabet is printed below to help, and as a clue you will need to shift each letter *forwards* through the alphabet to decode it – but never by more than 8 letters.

1) Tjp izzy oj adiy v cdyyzi gjxvodji

....

2) Wms amsjb zc y qcapcr yeclr

....

3) C xih'n fcey aynncha fimn

....

4) Owdd vgfw – Izak ak s ljaucq ugvw!

....

A B C D E F G H I J K L M N O P Q R S T U V W X Y Z

Seven words have been split in half, and their first halves placed in the left column and their second halves placed in the right column. Match the halves back up, forming all seven words without re-using any half. Be careful, since there are some incorrect matches that do form valid words but which won't let you complete the other words.

Once you have joined the pairs, read down the resulting words in the order of their left-hand halves, from top to bottom, to reveal a secret message.

LOC	ATE
SEC	DEN
PAP	DER
HID	ERS
INS	IDE
YEL	LOW
FOL	RET

What does the secret message say?

....

....

A secret message is hidden in the letter below, but you've got your hands on the secret key which will let you decrypt it:

4   1   4   6   4   5   2   10   9

Can you work out how to use it to reveal the message? Each of the numbers is identifying a *word* in the text, and notice how there are nine numbers in total. What are there also nine of in the text?

You are the only person who should read this letter. Open the second envelope when you have finished reading – it has more information. Did you find the keys I sent over? Please keep them in the safe place. Let me know when you have received this letter. I am counting on you to keep my secret! I have hidden some important items in a secret location. There is a map to find it, written on the back of this letter. Now you just have to figure out the password, and you'll be able to find it.

Can you crack the code to reveal a hidden five-letter word?

Each word below is missing its first and last letters, which **must be the same** – as for example in the word <u>W</u>INDO<u>W</u>. For each word, work out which one letter has been removed from the start and end, and write it in. A clue to each word is given.

Once you have worked out which letter is needed for each line, read those letters in order from top to bottom to reveal the hidden word.

.....HEELBARRO.....   Cart used by gardeners

.....RE.....   Width × height

.....OPSCOTC.....   Playground game with numbered boxes

.....REGAN.....   Herb used in cooking

.....SL.....   The capital city of Norway

What does the secret word say? ....

Can you spot a country hiding in each of the lines below?
As an example, the country CHAD is hidden in
'I gave the wit**ch a d**reamcatcher'.

All of the hidden country names have **four letters**. If you need
help, there's a list of all the four-letter countries in the world at
the bottom of the page.

1) I ran a marathon over the weekend.

    ....

2) The baby antelope runs towards its mother.

    ....

3) The decorators gave the bathroom a new coat of paint.

    ....

4) I don't want to go to school.

    ....

Four-letter countries:
Chad, Cuba, Fiji, Iran, Iraq, Laos, Mali, Niue,
Oman, Peru, and Togo

Starting at the grey square, can you work out how to use the following 'initial coded instructions' to trace a path and reveal a secret message hidden in the grid?

Note that there are 15 letters in the grid, and 15 words in the coded instructions. Is that a clue? Also, notice that many of the words start with the same letter.

Initial coded instructions:
Dreams reveal unusual robots riding dirty lorries down lowly lit driveways: red robots rampage unskilfully

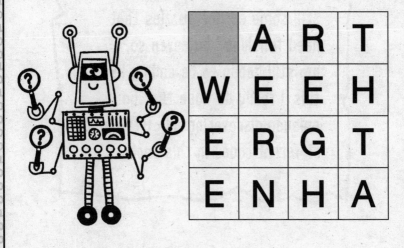

	A	R	T
W	E	E	H
E	R	G	T
E	N	H	A

What does the secret message say?

....

....

Can you reveal the hidden message in this 'final word' code?

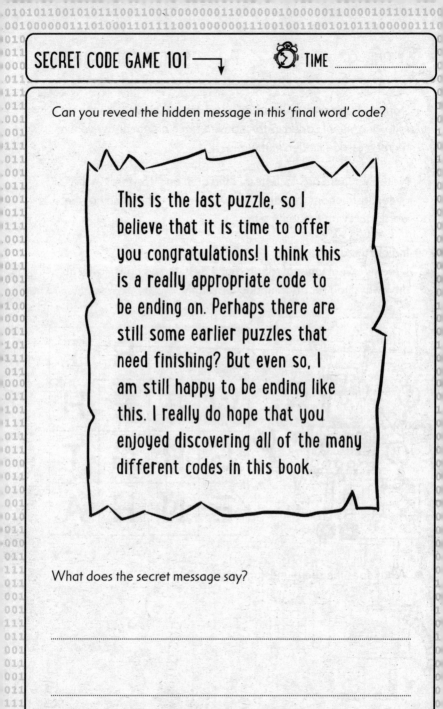

> This is the last puzzle, so I
> believe that it is time to offer
> you congratulations! I think this
> is a really appropriate code to
> be ending on. Perhaps there are
> still some earlier puzzles that
> need finishing? But even so, I
> am still happy to be ending like
> this. I really do hope that you
> enjoyed discovering all of the many
> different codes in this book.

What does the secret message say?

....

....

All
of the
ANSWERS

SECRET CODE GAME 1

1) Take
2) The
3) Train
4) Three
5) Stops

The secret message reads 'TAKE THE TRAIN THREE STOPS'.

SECRET CODE GAME 2

OPEN
THE
THIRD
DOOR

The message is
'OPEN THE THIRD DOOR'.

SECRET CODE GAME 3

Each of the words becomes a new word:

1) DO
2) NOT
3) ACCEPT
4) ANY
5) BILLS

The secret message is read from top to bottom:
'DO NOT ACCEPT ANY BILLS'.

SECRET CODE GAME 4

The notes from left to right are C, A, F, E, spelling the location:
CAFE.

SECRET CODE GAME 5

1) You
2) Did
3) Well
4) With
5) This
6) Puzzle

The secret message is 'YOU DID WELL WITH THIS PUZZLE'.

SECRET CODE GAME 6

The secret message is 'EVERY CLOUD HAS A SILVER LINING'.

SECRET CODE GAME 7

1) LI**Z**ARD
2) **O**RANGUTAN
3) PEA**C**OCK
4) **K**OALA
5) ANT**E**ATER
6) Z**E**BRA
7) ELE**P**HANT
8) **P**ENGUIN
9) TIGE**R**

The secret word is ZOOKEEPER.

SECRET CODE GAME 8

Shade in the squares in the letter grid that are shaded in the second grid. This hides some of the letters, to reveal a hidden message:

G	O			O	D
		J	O		B
O				N	
T	H		I	S	
C	O	D			E

This reveals 'GOOD JOB ON THIS CODE'.

SECRET CODE GAME 9

S	C	T	A	R	E
A	E	R	T	S	C
R	A	C	E	T	S
T	S	E	R	C	A
C	T	A	S	E	R
E	R	S	C	A	T

The hidden word is SECRET.

SECRET CODE GAME 10

Read the *italic*, <u>underlined</u> and CAPITALIZED words to reveal 'DON'T TELL ANYONE ABOUT THIS PRIVATE MESSAGE'.

SECRET CODE GAME 11

The word 'up', 'down', 'left' and 'right' are hidden within the words

1) RIGHT: **right**fully
2) DOWN: splash**down**
3) RIGHT: out**righ**tly
4) RIGHT: copy**right**
5) UP: ketch**up**
6) UP: porc**up**ine
7) UP: bankr**up**t
8) LEFT: **left**overs

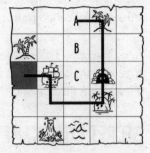

The path takes you to the letter 'A'.

SECRET CODE GAME 12

The following words cannot
be found in the grid:

- BRING
- EVERY
- PACKAGE
- THIS
- THURSDAY   So the secret message is
'BRING EVERY PACKAGE THIS THURSDAY'.

SECRET CODE GAME 13

1) TWO: Ar**two**rk
2) NINE: Brai**nine**ss
3) TEN: Ex**ten**t
4) EIGHT: H**eight**s
5) ONE: Teleph**one**s

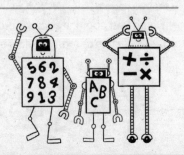

SECRET CODE GAME 14

Follow the arrows, square by square from the grey square, to trace the following path.

Read the letters along the path to reveal the secret message: 'FIND THE PINK FISH'.

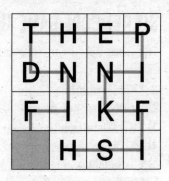

SECRET CODE GAME 15

Reading the first letter of each line reveals BUS STATION – which is where the secret meeting is taking place.

SECRET CODE GAME 16

1) now
2) you
3) can
4) read
5) in
6) the
7) dark

The message is 'NOW YOU CAN READ IN THE DARK' – which you could, if you were able to read Braille dots with your fingertips as many blind people can.

SECRET CODE GAME 17

All of the words have been written backwards. The messages are:

1) Deliver the note to the man dressed in red
2) Make sure nobody sees you
3) You will be given a secret name
4) You have ten minutes to complete the mission
5) Good luck with your important task

SECRET CODE GAME 18

- For a '+' symbol, add the lines from the second number to those in the first (in the same positions), so for example the 'I' and the 'Ч' make an 'H'.
- For a '−' symbol, erase the lines found in the second image from the first image (again in the same positions), so for example the 'I' removed from the 'B' leaves 'E'.

This results in:

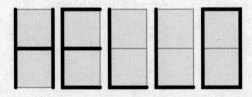

So the secret word is HELLO.

SECRET CODE GAME 19

1) MEET
2) ME
3) AT
4) THE
5) BANK

So the secret message is 'MEET ME AT THE BANK'.

SECRET CODE GAME 20

1) ROMEO: Are you travelling to **Rome, o**r Madrid?
2) ECHO: W**e cho**se the blue curtains.
3) VICTOR: Did the con**vict or**ganize his own escape?
4) ECHO: The scre**ech o**wl made a loud noise!
5) ALFA: The cow and her c**alf a**lways eat grass.
6) LIMA: Can you tel**l I'm a** bit nervous?

The secret word is REVEAL, which can be found by reading the first letter of each codeword in order from top to bottom.

SECRET CODE GAME 21

I have hidden the cash under the plant.
You will find it just inside the leaves.

SECRET CODE GAME 22

1) This
2) Code
3) Uses
4) Lots
5) Of
6) Flags

The secret message is 'THIS CODE USES LOTS OF FLAGS' – which is true!

SECRET CODE GAME 23

1) DIG = FIG
2) CHEERY - CHERRY
3) PRONE = PRUNE
4) LAME = LIME
5) DAZE = DATE

The secret word is FRUIT.

SECRET CODE GAME 24

The completed words are:
SCARE**S**
ENTIR**E**
COSMI**C**
REPAI**R**
EDIBL**E**
TEAPO**T**

The hidden word is SECRET.

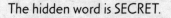

SECRET CODE GAME 25

1) Apple
2) Banana
3) Cherry
4) Date
5) Elderberry
6) Fig

Each is a fruit that begins with each letter of the alphabet in turn: A, B, C, and so on, so the seventh fruit should begin with 'G'. An example would be 'grape', which is '--· ·-· ·- ·--· ·' in Morse code.

SECRET CODE GAME 26

FI-ND
EA-CH
TI-NY
WO-RD

The hidden message is 'FIND EACH TINY WORD'.

SECRET CODE GAME 27

1) Meeting is tonight
2) The password is 'bananas'
3) Tap three times on the door

SECRET CODE GAME 28

THE	ENVELOPE	
YOU	NEED IS	
IN	BERLIN	

The message is 'THE ENVELOPE YOU NEED IS IN BERLIN'.

SECRET CODE GAME 29

All of the words have been reflected, as though they are being viewed in a mirror placed at the top of the page. Here's what the words look like when the entire page is viewed in such a mirror — which means that the words are now also written in reverse order:

WHO

HID

WHICH

ICE POP

So the message is 'WHO HID WHICH ICE POP?' and you could have read the message using a mirror.

SECRET CODE GAME 30

1) RED: Are you su**re d**ogs only sleep at night?
2) WHITE: The magic arro**w hit e**very target.
3) GREEN: The o**gre en**joyed eating mushrooms.
4) INDIGO: When there's lots of w**ind, I go** inside to keep warm.

SECRET CODE GAME 31

The notes from left to right are B, A, D, G and E – spelling BADGE.

SECRET CODE GAME 32

1) Wear
2) A
3) Blue
4) Ribbon
5) Today

The secret message reads 'WEAR A BLUE RIBBON TODAY'.

SECRET CODE GAME 33

L	N	A	O	P	D
P	O	D	N	L	A
D	L	N	P	A	O
A	P	O	D	N	L
N	D	L	A	O	P
O	A	P	L	D	N

The hidden location is LONDON.

SECRET CODE GAME 34

Each of the words becomes a new word:

1) HINT
2) BEGIN
3) BELOW
4) FIRST
5) DOOR

The secret message can be read by combining these words with the punctuation already on the page from top to bottom, to make 'HINT: BEGIN BELOW, FIRST DOOR'.

SECRET CODE GAME 35

1) this
2) code
3) must
4) be
5) read
6) by
7) hand

The message is 'THIS CODE MUST BE READ BY HAND' – which is exactly how Braille is designed to be read, by using your finger to read raised dots on a page.

SECRET CODE GAME 36

The first and second letters of each word have been swapped.
The messages are:

1) Come to the office before midnight
2) The next bus to arrive takes you abroad
3) Remember to wear yellow gloves
4) Make sure every puzzle has been solved
5) This is the final code of this type

SECRET CODE GAME 37

Each word has a set of double letters in it, which is the 'double agent' referred to.

- Fu**nn**y
- Hawa**ii**
- A**cc**ept
- Gr**ee**n

- Thr**ee**
- Stu**ff**
- Pu**ff**y
- Sp**oo**n
- Be**rr**y
- Be**tt**er

Read in order from top to bottom, they spell NICE EFFORT
– which also has a 'double agent' all of its own!

SECRET CODE GAME 38

1) Try
2) To
3) Keep
4) Your
5) Arms
6) Still

The secret message is 'TRY TO KEEP YOUR ARMS STILL'
– which is important for anyone using semaphore, other than
when they're actually using them to signal a letter.

SECRET CODE GAME 39

1) CAN**A**DA
2) PORT**U**GAL
3) **S**PAIN
4) ARGEN**T**INA
5) ALGE**R**IA
6) J**A**PAN
7) VENEZUE**L**A
8) THAI**L**AND
9) VIETN**A**M

The secret word is AUSTRALIA.

SECRET CODE GAME 40

1) ··· = S
2) – = T
3) · – · = R
4) – – – = O
5) – · = N
6) – – · = G

The secret word is STRONG.

SECRET CODE GAME 41

The secret message is
'OPEN THE GREEN DOOR AND FIND OUT'.

SECRET CODE GAME 42

1) Wait
2) Until
3) The
4) High
5) Speed
6) Train
7) Arrives

The secret message is
'WAIT UNTIL THE HIGH-SPEED
TRAIN ARRIVES'.

SECRET CODE GAME 43

1) CAT: Lo**cat**e
2) LION: Mil**lion**s
3) SEAL: Re**seal**ed
4) OWL: Gr**owl**ed
5) FISH: Unsel**fish**ly

SECRET CODE GAME 44

The letters can be interpreted as compass directions: N=north, E=east, S=south, W=west. Follow these, square by square from the grey square, to trace the following path:

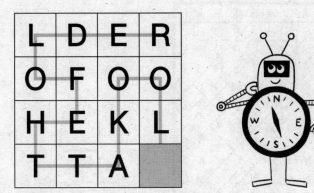

Read the letters along the path to reveal the secret message: 'LOOK AT THE FOLDER'.

SECRET CODE GAME 45

The following words cannot be found in the grid:

- ALWAYS
- CONCEAL
- DIRECTIONS
- PROPERLY
- USING
- WORDS

So the secret message is 'ALWAYS CONCEAL DIRECTIONS PROPERLY USING WORDS'.

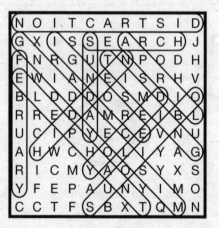

SECRET CODE GAME 46

1) **S.** The sequence is numbers written as words – One, Two, Three, Four, Five, Six – so the next number is Seven.
2) **U.** The sequence is planets in order from the sun outwards – Mercury, Venus, Earth, Mars, Jupiter, Saturn – so the next planet is Uranus.

SECRET CODE GAME 47

LO-OK
WI-TH
YO-UR
EY-ES
ON-LY

The hidden message is 'LOOK WITH YOUR EYES ONLY'.

SECRET CODE GAME 48

1) LOOK: to make OVERLOOK and LOOKALIKE
2) OUT: to make HIDEOUT and OUTSIDE
3) FISH: to make GOLDFISH and FISHBOWL
4) IN: to make WITHIN and INDEED
5) WATER: to make RAINWATER and WATERFALL

The hidden message is 'LOOK OUT: FISH IN WATER'.

SECRET CODE GAME 49

- For a '+' symbol, add the lines from the second number to those in the first (in the same positions), so for example the 'ι' and the '˥' make an 'ɴ'. (For the second line, add the lines from both numbers to the lines of the first number)
- For a '−' symbol, erase the lines found in the second image from the first image (again in the same positions), so for example the 'ι' removed from the 'B' leaves 'E'.

This results in the word CANCEL:

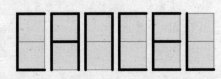

SECRET CODE GAME 50

The words 'up', 'down', 'left' and 'right' are hidden within the words:

1) UP: c**up**board
2) UP: p**up**py
3) RIGHT: f**right**en
4) UP: so**up**
5) RIGHT: b**right**ly
6) RIGHT: al**right**
7) DOWN: lan**down**er
8) DOWN: eider**down**
9) LEFT: c**left**

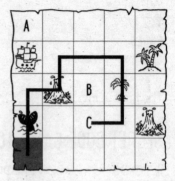

The path takes you to the letter 'C'.

SECRET CODE GAME 51

The completed words are:

STONE**S**
MEDIU**M**
ALPAC**A**
RICHE**R**
TALEN**T**

The hidden word is SMART.

SECRET CODE GAME 52

1) River
2) Ocean
3) Mountain
4) Sea
5) Lake
6) Lagoon

All of the words are natural water features, except for 'mountain'.

SECRET CODE GAME 53

YOU MUST ONLY USE THE SILVER KEY

The message is 'YOU MUST ONLY USE THE SILVER KEY'.

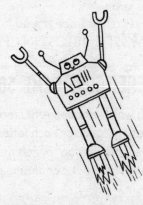

SECRET CODE GAME 54

1) Eye
2) Level
3) Radar
4) Noon
5) Hello
6) Kayak

All of the words can be read either forwards or backwards (that is, are palindromes) — except for 'hello'.

SECRET CODE GAME 55

Each of the words becomes a new word:

1) ALMOST
2) GOT
3) LOST
4) IN
5) CHILLY
6) HILLS

The secret message is read from top to bottom:
'ALMOST GOT LOST IN CHILLY HILLS'.

SECRET CODE GAME 56

Each word has been reflected so it is written backwards, using a variety of fonts for each letter. Reflecting each word back to its normal orientation reveals the message 'CRACK SECRET CODES', writing it without a confusing mix of upper- and lower-case letters.

SECRET CODE GAME 57

1) LOOK: LOOKOUT, LOOKALIKE, LOOKUP
2) FOR: FORBIDDEN, FORGIVE, FORTUNE
3) ANY: ANYBODY, ANYTIME, ANYTHING
4) GREEN: GREENHOUSE, GREENFLY, GREENGROCER
5) CAR: CARROT, CARPET, CARTON

The message is 'LOOK OUT FOR ANY GREEN CAR'.

SECRET CODE GAME 58

1) t
2) o
3) u
4) c
5) h

The hidden word is TOUCH — which is what you use to read Braille.

SECRET CODE GAME 59

The first and last letters of each word have been swapped.
The messages are:

1) The green car will take you to the hotel
2) Wait inside the restaurant until midday
3) A secret agent will give you important papers
4) You are doing excellent work
5) Well done for cracking the code

SECRET CODE GAME 60

1) MAXI = **T**AXI
2) TEAM = T**R**AM
3) COUCH = CO**A**CH
4) BAN = **V**AN
5) PLANT = PLAN**E**
6) TRAINER = TRAI**L**ER

The secret word is TRAVEL.

SECRET CODE GAME 61

1) **S**TAR – ART
2) **P**EARL – REAL
3) TEAS**I**NG – AGENTS
4) H**E**ADS – DASH
5) **S**TABLE – BLEAT

The word that remains is SPIES.

SECRET CODE GAME 62

The four words can be found by
reading downwards. If you take the
first letter of each row, they spell
BLUE. The second letters spell PINK.
The third letters spell GOLD. The
final letters spell CYAN.

SECRET CODE GAME 63

1) Find the woman with the red hat (Shift backwards by 1)
2) You are an excellent code cracker (Shift backwards by 3)
3) Hannah is not my real name (Shift backwards by 2)
4) I like to travel and solve mysteries (Shift backwards by 4)

SECRET CODE GAME 64

The notes from left to right are C, A, B, B, A, G and E – spelling CABBAGE. What a great thing to hide a secret message in!

SECRET CODE GAME 65

The code works by counting the number of sides on each shape. This number then tells you which letter to choose according to its position in the alphabet.

A triangle has 3 sides, and letter 3 in the alphabet is C – so a triangle represents C, a square represents D, and so on.

1) HIDE
2) EDGE

SECRET CODE GAME 66

1) PAPA: We stopped to hel**p a pa**ir of old ladies.
2) HOTEL: The sports hots**hot el**bowed his teammate.
3) OSCAR: I dreamed I saw two flaming**os car**rying handbags.
4) TANGO: Which way did the orangu**tan go**?
5) OSCAR: I don't want t**o scar**e the new puppy.

The secret word is PHOTO, which can be found by reading the first letter of each codeword in order from top to bottom.

SECRET CODE GAME 67

ALW-AYS
DEC-ODE
EMA-ILS
DUR-ING
ONL-INE
QUE-STS

The hidden message is
'ALWAYS DECODE EMAILS DURING ONLINE QUESTS'.

SECRET CODE GAME 68

D	S	R	A	E	V	T	I	L
V	E	T	L	I	D	A	S	R
A	I	L	T	R	S	E	D	V
R	T	A	I	D	L	S	V	E
S	L	E	R	V	A	D	T	I
I	V	D	S	T	E	L	R	A
E	D	S	V	L	I	R	A	T
L	R	I	D	A	T	V	E	S
T	A	V	E	S	R	I	L	D

The hidden word is DELIVERED.

SECRET CODE GAME 69

1) **T**RAIN
2) CA**R**
3) BO**A**T
4) U**N**ICYCLE
5) **S**HIP
6) **P**LANE
7) SCO**O**TER
8) FE**R**RY
9) **T**RAM

The secret word is TRANSPORT.

SECRET CODE GAME 70

1) Octopus
2) Jellyfish
3) Shark
4) Whale
5) Eagle
6) Lobster

All of the words are animals which live underwater,
except for 'eagle'.

SECRET CODE GAME 71

The secret message is
'THE PLANE WILL LAND AT
SIX TOMORROW MORNING'.

SECRET CODE GAME 72

1) DAISY: The anacon**da is y**ellowy-brown, with dark spots.
2) IRIS: The armcha**ir I s**it in at the library is really comfy.
3) LILY: Is there any brocco**li ly**ing in the shopping basket?
4) ORCHID: Don't bring a t**orch – I d**on't think you'll need one.

SECRET CODE GAME 73

1) SEE: SEEKING, SEESAW, SEEMED
2) BLUE: BLUEBERRY, BLUEBIRD, BLUEBELL
3) BOOK: BOOKMARK, BOOKSHELF, BOOKCASE
4) UNDER: UNDERWATER, UNDERSTAND, UNDERCOVER
5) STEP: STEPLADDER, STEPBROTHER, STEPMOTHER

The message is 'SEE BLUE BOOK UNDER STEP'.

SECRET CODE GAME 74

The revealed letters are E, A, S and Y – spelling EASY.

SECRET CODE GAME 75

Each sentence has been written backwards. The messages are:

1) Try and hide behind that tree
2) You should wear sunglasses as a disguise
3) Your code name is 'blue banana'
4) Look under the sofa for a bunch of keys
5) Congratulations on this excellent code cracking

SECRET CODE GAME 76

1) **V.** The sequence is the rainbow in order – Red, Orange, Yellow, Green, Blue, Indigo – so the next is Violet.
2) **J.** The sequence is months of the year in calendar order – January, February, March, April, May, June – so the next month is July.

SECRET CODE GAME 77

The message reads 'TIME FOR THE PACKAGE EXCHANGE'.

SECRET CODE GAME 78

The completed words are:

CHOCAHOLI**C**
HAIRBRUS**H**
ANACOND**A**
MUSEU**M**
PARSNI**P**

The hidden word is CHAMP.

SECRET CODE GAME 79

Each letter has been reflected. Reflecting each letter back to its normal orientation reveals the message 'BRING SEVEN LEMONS'.

SECRET CODE GAME 80

- For a '+' symbol, add the lines from the second number to those in the first (in the same positions), so for example the 'I' and the 'Ч' make an 'H'.
- For a '–' symbol, erase the lines found in the second image from the first image (again in the same positions), so for example the 'I' removed from the 'B' leaves 'E'.

So the hidden word is CHOICE:

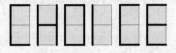

SECRET CODE GAME 81

1) ·· — · = F
2) ·· = I
3) · = E
4) · — ·· = L
5) — ·· = D

The secret word is FIELD.

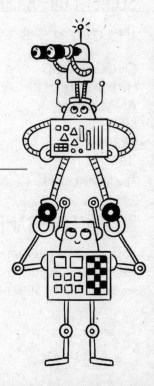

SECRET CODE GAME 82

1. <u>M</u>AILED – IDEAL
2. GRA<u>I</u>N – RANG
3. HOR<u>S</u>E – HERO
4. <u>S</u>INGER – REIGN
5. ADM<u>I</u>RE – DREAM
6. LISTE<u>N</u> – TILES
7. BAD<u>G</u>ER – BREAD

The word that remains is MISSING.

SECRET CODE GAME 83

1) DO: to make UNDO and DOME
2) NOT: to make CANNOT and NOTICE
3) USE: to make REFUSE and USELESS
4) RED: to make COVERED and REDRAW
5) KEY: to make DONKEY and KEYBOARD

The hidden message is 'DO NOT USE RED KEY'.

SECRET CODE GAME 84

1) $- \cdot \cdot \cdot = B$
2) $\cdot - \cdot = R$
3) $\cdot = E$
4) $\cdot - = A$
5) $- \cdot \cdot = D$

So the secret password is BREAD.

SECRET CODE GAME 85

The code works by counting the number of sides on each shape. This number then tells you which letter to choose according to its position in the alphabet, as in puzzle 1.

A triangle has 3 sides, and letter 3 in the alphabet is C — so a triangle represents C, a square represents D, and so on.

1) CHIEF
2) DECIDE

SECRET CODE GAME 86

WELL DONE
YOU HAVE
COMPLETED
THE SECRET
OPERATION

The message is 'WELL DONE YOU HAVE COMPLETED THE SECRET OPERATION'.

SECRET CODE GAME 87

- For a '+' symbol, add the lines from the second number to those in the first (in the same positions), so for example the '|' and the '⅂' make an 'ᒠ'.
- For a '-' symbol, erase the lines found in the second image from the first image (again in the same positions), so for example the '|' removed from the 'B' leaves 'E'.

So the hidden word is SENSIBLE:

SECRET CODE GAME 88

1) Red
2) Dear
3) Adore
4) Soared
5) Roasted
6) Asteroid
7) Dreamiest

Each word uses the same letters as the previous word plus one extra, although in a different order. However, 'Dreamiest' breaks this rule and so is the odd one out since it's missing the 'o' that it should have had from 'asteroid'.

SECRET CODE GAME 89

O	E	V	S	B	D	A	T	R
D	B	T	A	V	R	S	E	O
A	R	S	O	E	T	V	B	D
V	D	O	E	T	S	R	A	B
B	A	E	D	R	O	T	S	V
S	T	R	B	A	V	D	O	E
R	O	D	T	S	B	E	V	A
E	S	B	V	D	A	O	R	T
T	V	A	R	O	E	B	D	S

The hidden word is OBSERVERS.

SECRET CODE GAME 90

1) Cuba
2) Italy
3) France
4) Bolivia
5) Paraguay
6) Indonesia

Each is a country that has one more letter than
the previous one, so the seventh country should have
ten letters. An example would be 'Mozambique', which is
'-- --- --●● ●- -- -●●● ●● --●- ●●- ●'
in Morse code.

SECRET CODE GAME 91

The revealed letters are S, I, G and N – spelling SIGN.

SECRET CODE GAME 92

The corresponding Braille characters
for each letter look like this:

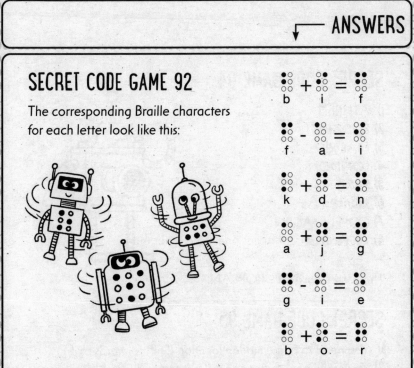

$$b + i = f$$

$$f - a = i$$

$$k + d = n$$

$$a + j = g$$

$$g - i = e$$

$$b + o = r$$

So the hidden word is FINGER – which is what you would use to
read Braille.

SECRET CODE GAME 93

The sums can be solved as follows:

1+2=3 14-2=12 2+3=5 21+1=22 7-2=5 9+9=18

15+4=19 20-5=15 7+5=12 11×2=22 4+5=9 2×7=14 1×7=7

These numbers can then be converted to letters using A=1, B=2,
C=3 and so on:

3=C 12=L 5=E 22=V 5=E 18=R

19=S 15=O 12=L 22=V 9=I 14=N 7=G

… so the message reads CLEVER SOLVING.

SECRET CODE GAME 94

1) AT**H**ENS
2) B**U**DAPEST
3) MAD**R**ID
4) L**O**NDON
5) **P**ARIS
6) ROM**E**
7) COPENH**A**GEN
8) VIE**N**NA

The secret word is EUROPEAN.

SECRET CODE GAME 95

1) You need to find a hidden location (Shift forwards by 5)
2) You could be a secret agent (Shift forwards 2)
3) I don't like getting lost (Shift forwards 6)
4) Well done – this is a tricky code! (Shift forwards by 8)

SECRET CODE GAME 96

LOC-ATE
SEC-RET
PAP-ERS
HID-DEN
INS-IDE
YEL-LOW
FOL-DER

The hidden message is
'LOCATE SECRET PAPERS HIDDEN INSIDE YELLOW FOLDER'.

SECRET CODE GAME 97

There are nine numbers and nine sentences, and each number refers to a different sentence. The number tells you which word to pick from each sentence, where 1 is the 1st word, 2 is the 2nd word, and so on. Therefore the secret message is 'ONLY OPEN THE SAFE WHEN YOU HAVE THE PASSWORD'.

'You are the **only** person who should read this letter. **Open** the second envelope when you have finished reading – it has more information. Did you find **the** keys I sent over? Please keep them in the **safe** place. Let me know **when** you have received this letter. I am counting on **you** to keep my secret! I **have** hidden some important items in a secret location. There is a map to find it, written on **the** back of this letter. Now you just have to figure out the **password**, and you'll be able to find it.'

SECRET CODE GAME 98

The completed words are:

WHEELBARRO**W**
ARE**A**
HOPSCOTC**H**
OREGAN**O**
OSL**O**

The hidden word is WAHOO!

SECRET CODE GAME 99

1) IRAN: **I ran** a marathon over the weekend.
2) PERU: The baby antelo**pe ru**ns towards its mother.
3) OMAN: The decorators gave the bathro**om a n**ew coat of paint.
4) TOGO: I don't want **to go** to school.

SECRET CODE GAME 100

Each word in the instructions starts with one of 'u', 'd', 'l' or 'r' –
which should be interpreted as up, down, left or right respectively.
Follow these, square by square from the grey square, to trace the
following path:

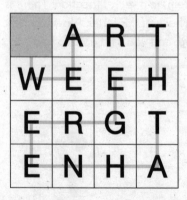

Read the letters along the path to reveal the secret message
'WEAR THE GREEN HAT'.

SECRET CODE GAME 101

Read the last (or 'final') word in each sentence, to reveal
'CONGRATULATIONS ON FINISHING THIS BOOK'.
And congratulations indeed – you're now a master codebreaker!

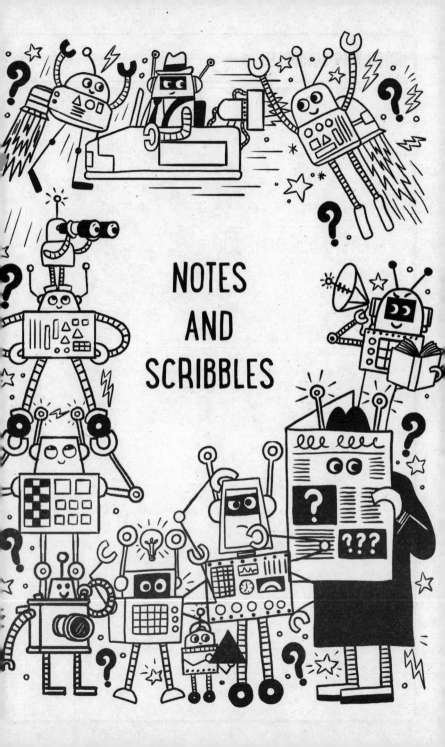

NOTES
AND
SCRIBBLES

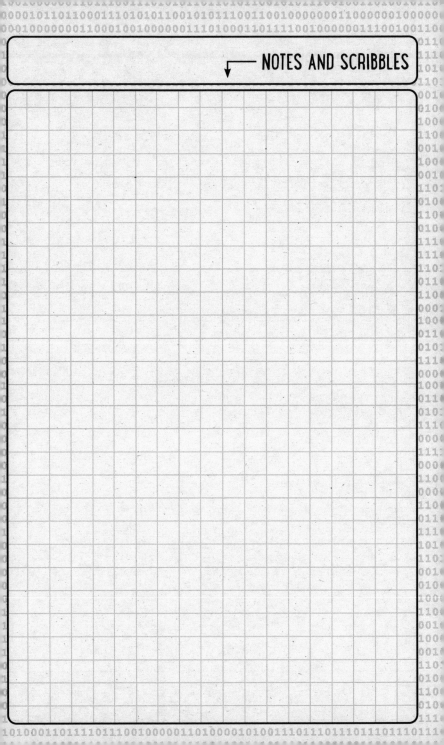

NOTES AND SCRIBBLES →

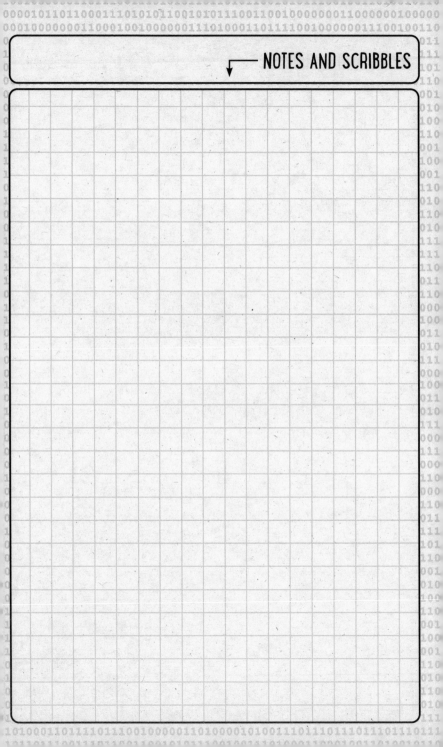

SECRET
CODE
GUIDE

Musical notes are each given a letter from A to G, each of which corresponds with a different musical pitch. These then repeat continually, so once you go past G you come back round to A.

Musical notes can be drawn as markings on a set of horizontal lines, like the ones below. The horizontal lines together form a 'stave'. The exact note that each mark corresponds to depends on which line it crosses, or on which two lines it is in between. It also depends on the clef that is being used, which is the swirly symbol at the very start of the stave.

In the picture below, seven notes on the treble clef stave are shown. The letters that correspond to each note are also marked below. Usually these notes are used when making music, but in this book you can use the letters that correspond to each note in order to decode hidden messages!

F G A B C D E

Treble clef

SECRET CODE GUIDE: THE BRAILLE ALPHABET

The Braille alphabet is a way of writing letters so they can be read by blind or partially sighted people. Each letter is converted into a pattern of dots, and then these dots are pushed into the surface of a piece of paper so that someone can read them using their fingertip to feel which dots are there. All of the patterns are based on a 2×3 grid, and the top row always has at least one dot in it so that it's always clear where each pattern starts. For the same reason, if the dot in the first row is in the second column then there must always be a dot somewhere else in the first column.

It's amazing that you can learn to read with just your fingertips, and if you ever come across Braille yourself — as you might for example on a museum exhibit — then if you give it a go you'll see just how tricky it is to feel each of the dot patterns. But with practice it's possible to be able to read Braille really quickly.

In this book there are no raised dots, but instead each Braille letter is shown with a picture like those on the opposite page. A black dot represents a raised dot, and the white dots are just there to help keep track of things — in actual Braille there would simply be a gap where there's a white dot in this book.

The Braille Alphabet

A	⠁	J	⠚	S	⠎
B	⠃	K	⠅	T	⠞
C	⠉	L	⠇	U	⠥
D	⠙	M	⠍	V	⠧
E	⠑	N	⠝	W	⠺
F	⠋	O	⠕	X	⠭
G	⠛	P	⠏	Y	⠽
H	⠓	Q	⠟	Z	⠵
I	⠊	R	⠗		

SECRET CODE GUIDE: CAESAR SHIFT ⟶

A Caeser shift cipher is a simple method of changing the letters you use to write a message so that it becomes harder to read. It get its name from the Roman emperor, Julius Caesar, who used a similar code. He lived over 2,000 years ago, so it's a code that's been around for a long time!

In a Caesar shift, each letter is 'shifted' by a fixed amount through the alphabet. So, for example, if each letter was shifted one place through the alphabet then an 'A' would become a 'B', and a 'B' would become a 'C', and so on. If you wanted to write the word 'cab', then with a Caesar shift of one it would become 'dbc', since each letter has then been shifted forward one place through the alphabet. Letters that shift off the end of the alphabet simply 'wrap around' to the other end, so for example a 'Z' with a shift of one would become an 'A'.

Letters can be shifted forwards or backwards, so just as a forward shift of one turns an 'A' into a 'B', so a backward shift of one would turn an 'A' into a 'Z'. To decipher a Caesar shift code, therefore, you just apply the opposite shift – so if it was encoded with a forward shift of five, you would decode it with a backwards shift of five.

Caesar Shift Wheel

Use the following wheel of letters to decode a Caesar shift message. Start at the letter you want to decode, then count forward or backward around the wheel by the given number of steps to get to the decoded letter. You could also use the wheel to encode a message too, if you wanted.

backward

forward

V W X Y Z A B C D E F G H I J K L M N O P Q R S T U

SECRET CODE GUIDE: MORSE CODE ⟶

Morse code is a simple method for sending letters and numbers by using a mix of two different signal durations, known as 'dots' (for a short signal) and 'dashes' (for a long signal).

In this book there are no signals being transmitted, so the dots and dashes are represented with *actual* dots and dashes: '•' and '-'. Different combinations of dots and dashes make up different characters, as shown on the page opposite. Pauses between signals — or extra spaces in this book — are used to separate one letter from the next.

Morse code was first used all the way back in 1844 to send telegraph messages, which used a single electrical wire. All that could be sent down the wire was an electronic 'on' or 'off', so by tapping on a single button at one end — and listening to the resulting short and long sounds at the other end — Morse code could be used to send text. Thanks to this system, messages were able to be sent immediately over long distances, including overseas. Back in the 19th century this was an enormous leap forward in communications technology.

Morse code can be sent via any on/off method, so another way it can be sent is by turning a light on and off. Short flashes represent dots, and long flashes represent dashes.

Morse code table

A •-	M --	Y -•--
B -•••	N -•	Z --••
C -•-•	O ---	1 •----
D -••	P •--•	2 ••---
E •	Q --•-	3 •••--
F ••-•	R •-•	4 ••••-
G --•	S •••	5 •••••
H ••••	T -	6 -••••
I ••	U ••-	7 --•••
J •---	V •••-	8 ---••
K -•-	W •--	9 ----•
L •-••	X -••-	0 -----

SECRET CODE GUIDE: RADIO CODEWORDS →

If you've ever tried to spell out a word to someone else, you'll know that it's easy to mishear certain letters. For example, an 'S' and an 'F' can sometimes sound very similar, especially if you're talking over a poor quality phone line, or are in a noisy room. Usually this doesn't matter too much, but in certain circumstances it's really important that there can be no confusion over which letters are being spoken. To get around this problem, radio codewords were invented. They're called 'radio' codewords because they were designed to be transmitted over a radio signal, such as between a pair of walkie-talkies.

In English, the radio codewords are defined by the 'NATO Phonetic Alphabet', which is shown on the opposite page. To use it, you simply replace each letter that you want to spell with its associated codeword. So, instead of saying 'S' you would simply say 'Sierra' instead. Of it someone says 'Sierra' to you then you know that they actually mean 'S'.

The codewords were chosen so that they don't sound very similar, which means it should be much harder for anyone to mishear you. You could try it out next time you need to spell out a word to someone, if you like!

SECRET CODE GUIDE: RADIO CODEWORDS

Radio codewords

A – Alfa*

B – Bravo

C – Charlie

D – Delta

E – Echo

F – Foxtrot

G – Golf

H – Hotel

I – India

J – Juliett

K – Kilo

L – Lima

M – Mike

N – November

O – Oscar

P – Papa

Q – Quebec

R – Romeo

S – Sierra

T – Tango

U – Uniform

V – Victor

W – Whiskey

X – X-ray

Y – Yankee

Z – Zulu

*Note that the word for 'A', 'alfa', is sometimes also written as 'alpha' – but both mean the same.

SECRET CODE GUIDE: SEMAPHORE LETTERS ⟶

Semaphore is a way of holding flags in order to send a message. Somebody holds a flag in their left hand and another flag in their right hand, then points each hand in one of eight directions: up, down, left, right and the four main diagonal directions between them. Each different combination of flags represents a different letter, as shown on the page opposite.

Semaphore was mostly used to send messages from ship to ship, when they were at sea but not so far apart that they could not see each other. It didn't require any equipment at all, other than the two flags, so it was very simple to use.

Semaphore letters

A		J		S	
B		K		T	
C		L		U	
D		M		V	
E		N		W	
F		O		X	
G		P		Y	
H		Q		Z	
I		R			

ALSO AVAILABLE:

ISBN 9781780558882

ISBN 9781780559155

ISBN 9781780558264

ISBN 9781780558721

ISBN 9781780557403

ISBN 9781780557106

ISBN 9781780556642

ISBN 9781780556635

ISBN 9781780556628

ISBN 9781780556543

ISBN 9781780556659

ISBN 9781780556192

ISBN 9781780556185

ISBN 9781780556208

ISBN 9781780555935

ISBN 9781780555638

ISBN 9781780554730

ISBN 9781780555621

ISBN 9781780554723

ISBN 9781780555409

ISBN 9781780553146

ISBN 9781780553085

ISBN 9781780553078

ISBN 9781780552491